How to Repair Furniture

by

RAYMOND F. YATES

Nicholas Kaye · · London

First published in Great Britain by Nicholas Kaye, Ltd.,
Trebeck Street, London, W.1. 1950

PRINTED FOR NICHOLAS KAYE LTD.
AT THE YORKDALE PRESS,
THORNTON ROAD, BRADFORD.

CONTENTS

THE TOOL KIT AND ITS USE

There is a temptation for beginners who can afford it to go all out on the purchase of home workshop tools both hand and power. In the humble opinion of this writer, a beginner's shop full of luxurious and expensive tools is a mistake and an encumbrance. Many such shops are set up by men who, in truth, do not yet know how properly to use a screwdriver. One sees them in the act of attempting to drive home a 2-inch wood screw with a driver tip that does not fit the screw slot and that is either too large or too small for the job at hand. It is one thing to own a fine set of tools and quite another thing to acquire the skill to make the most of it.

Regardless of the funds one has available for the purchase of tools, it is recommended that only the minimum requirements be supplied at first. Such an outfit amounts to a challenge to its owner. Things made with it, or repair and restoration jobs done with it, reflect great credit on the craftsman. Any tinker, no matter how rank, can split a pencil line on a £20 circular saw but the fellow who can do it with a handsaw has more claim to pride. There is a pleasure, a peculiar satisfaction, that comes from skill supplied by the hands rather than those made easily possible by a machine. That does not put a curse on the latter but it does point to the desirability of a good sound training with hand tools before one graduates to power-driven saws, planers, drills, sanders and the like.

For the reasons already stated, this book will have little to say concerning the home shop woodworking machine because any of the operations described herein may be done by machine as well as with the hand tool recommended in the list soon to follow.

In making purchases of tools, let the beginner beware of the fact that all that glitters is not good steel. A lot of gaudy trash in the way of tools is reaching the market to-day. It is to be avoided. A bit of chromium and a red or blue plastic handle may easily hide a piece of junk. One would rather purchase a single good chisel than a half dozen poor ones that will not hold their edges. In short, one does not want to buy the mass production stuff. Rather one wants the finer tools even though it takes one longer and costs more to put a set together. Work will be better, take less time and produce less impatience.

The list of needed things follows: —

      1 claw hammer of best quality
      1 wooden or plastic head mallet
      1 set wood chisels—$\frac{1}{8}$, $\frac{1}{4}$, $\frac{3}{8}$, $\frac{1}{2}$, $\frac{5}{8}$, $\frac{3}{4}$, $\frac{7}{8}$ and 1 inch
      1 set of at least five screwdrivers from light to heavy
      1 set of bits—$\frac{1}{4}$ to 1 inch in eighths
      2 oilstones—one medium, one fine
      1 folding rule
      1 marking gauge
      1 hand drill
      1 good quality (bit) brace
      1 small square
      1 large square
      1 marking knife
      1 jack plane
      1 block plane
      1 smoothing plane
      1 set wood scrapers (see later remarks)

1 back saw
1 mitre box, made or purchased
1 coping saw
1 compass saw (wrongly called keyhole)
1 drawknife (optional)
1 spokeshave
1 crosscut saw
1 ripsaw
1 set of nail sets
1 wood rasp
1 cabinet scraper
1 set 4-inch clamps

This list could be greatly extended but as a beginner's outfit the tools included above are sufficient. If the cost is too great to be borne in one lump sum, then one chisel, one plane, one screwdriver, etc., may be purchased at a time. In no event should the worker give in to the temptation to purchase a complete set of the gaudier and cheaper tools, however glowing the terms of the advertisements or counter-cards.

A good workbench is expensive, especially those with laminated hardwood tops. One does not need such fancy things. A bench made up of pine or spruce planks two inches thick is perfectly satisfactory. The legs, as well as the bracing cross members, may be 2 x 4. A very simple home-made workbench is shown in Fig. 1.

In making this bench the mistake of using nails is to be avoided. It must be remembered that any workbench is subjected to considerable lateral strain, as when one is planing, for instance. Even though cut nails are used in making such a bench, they will eventually work loose. This calls for still more nails and soon it is found that the 2 x 4s are splitting and that is the end of the bench.

All of this trouble can be avoided for the period of a

lifetime if in place of the spikes or nails the worker uses ¼-inch coach bolts pulled up tight. The holes are drilled with a ¼-inch twist-bit which produces a tight fit and makes for rigidity. Three-eighths inch bolts may be used on very heavy benches. Such bolts cost only a few pence each at any hardware store.

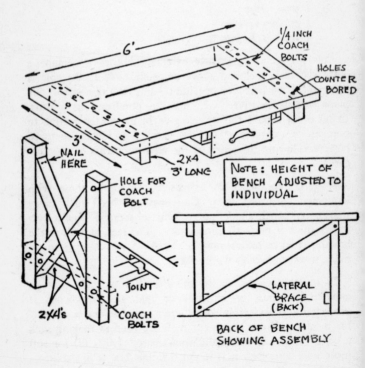

FIG. 1. This sturdy workbench can easily be made at home for about £1 or so, and from materials locally available.

It may be necessary to occasionally give the nuts of the coach bolts a turn or two to keep the bench rigid. It is assumed that a wood vice is attached to the bench.

An excellent and simple vice of this sort is pictured in Fig. 2. Any local plumber will make the metal part for a few shillings. This amounts largely to threading the pipe shaft.

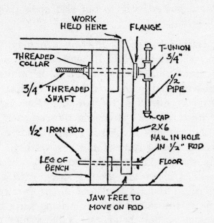

Fig. 2. Details of a good home-made vice for a woodworking bench. Metal materials are available at local plumbing shops.

The other plumbing articles involved are standard fittings costing only a few pence each. The movable jaw may be a piece of 2 x 6 rafter. It will be noticed that the lower end of the vice jaw is made so that it is adjustable to the thickness of the piece of wood being held. This is to provide the gripping end of the jaw with as much contacting surface as possible with the piece of wood being held. This prevents marking, especially in the case of soft pine.

The ordinary all-metal vice is not suited to wood working not only because of the metal jaws but also because of the height, which is awkward for planing, chiselling, etc.

Now that the tools needed are listed, it will be advisable to treat them one by one, commenting not only on their proper design features and adjustment but also upon proper use as well.

We will start with the hammer, which may sound disgustingly simple. But is it? If someone does not believe there can be much difference in hammers, let him attempt to drive a finishing nail with a ball peen hammer. Every mechanic has his own type of hammer, the engineer, the cobbler, the tinsmith, the mason and the carpenter. A good carpenter's hammer first of all has a head made of the right stuff—tempered forged steel of the best quality. The head is wedged to the handle properly and the handle is of fine, hard wood. The claws are ground sharp with a carefully proportioned V. The head is also of the proper weight with just the right curvature to the face (striking surface). Above all, the hammer is well balanced. Such a tool cannot be purchased for a shilling. It is more apt to cost four times this amount but such a tool will last a lifetime.

The rank amateur always reveals his training and skill in the manner in which he uses a hammer. Usually he grasps the handle in the middle which is awkward. In this he fails to take full advantage of the driving power of the tool; a simple matter of leverage. The handle should be gripped near its end. Nails should be started by one or two light blows. Then the head of the hammer is for an instant rested on the nailhead, as close to the centre of the former as possible. Withdrawn from this position, it is raised carefully and the first full blow struck. A little practise may be needed but soon the worker will be able to drive a nail quickly and accurately. Nails are bent before reaching home only because of inaccurate or semi-glancing blows. When hit fully and squarely they always go home straight unless the wrong nail is used. The nail may be too long or too small in diameter for the wood if it is hard. Hard wood requires more careful driving, easing up on the power of the blows. Sometimes a large number of small blows will drive a nail into hard wood whereas difficulty and bending would be had with heavy blows, especially those that might be delivered by an amateur.

The need for developing accuracy in striking will be appreciated in working with soft pine where the face of the hammer makes an ugly depression when the hammer head misses fire. These dimples left by the hammer cannot be removed and they mark a piece of work as coming from inexperienced hands. It is to be noted here that the face of the hammer is slightly convex for the purpose of driving the nail a slight distance below the surface of the wood in which it is used.

In using the claw for the extraction of bent nails, the worker should take the greatest possible advantage of all of the leverage the handle of the hammer can afford. One must also be careful that the back of the claw does not leave a mark on the wood. Considerable pressure may develop between the wood and the hammer head. Oftentimes a small piece of cardboard or a wooden block slipped between the two will prevent such marks, especially on soft wood.

In the case of extracting a nail driven almost home, a small block of wood is slipped under the hammer head after the nail has been pulled out an inch or so. This not only protects the wood but preserves the leverage for easy extraction. It is well, too, to jam the claw well into the body of the nail just below the head. This takes some of the strain off the head and may save it from being pulled off.

In the production of finished work where the driving of nails is followed by the use of the nail set and putty, the right nail set should be used on finishing nails. Two different sizes will be sufficient. The head of the nail need not be driven any more than ⅛ inch below the surface of the wood and the mechanic should be sure that the nail set is poised exactly on the top of the nail before he drives the blow which need be only a moderate one.

A perfectly tooled shop might boast of two claw hammers, a small one and a large one. For instance, if one were building a birdhouse of ¼-inch pine stock using 1½-inch finishing nails, a smaller claw hammer would be more convenient. It would, however, amount to a luxury.

Shame on the fellow caught using a claw hammer on a chisel! Such usage would immediately mark him as a hopeless tinker and a careless one. Chisel handles do not last long with such punishment. It is nice to have a wooden or plastic mallet about. It is also nice to have one of the newer rubber mallets when driving a tight fit on a recalcitrant piece of soft pine. This may be struck sharp blows with a rubber mallet without danger to the wood. Here again, a rubber mallet is a luxury although such a thing is not too expensive. As a substitute, one may use a block of wood and strike it with a claw hammer.

People who know what they are about purchase the best chisels money can buy. Better one good one than six that lose their edges with the first few blows from the mallet. Thereafter they chew and crush wood rather than cut it. The careful worker always keeps his oilstone at hand. In cutting hard wood, he may sharpen a chisel several times while making a deep cut, as in the case of a mortised joint where cutting across the grain is necessary and calls for all of the cutting power that even a sharp chisel may have.

Chisels come in three styles and in widths separated by eighths up to 1 inch. After that they come in widths advancing in quarters. The home shop will not need to go beyond a width of 2 inches. If only one chisel can be afforded at first, then that one should be ½ inch. It is nice to have a set of seven chisels from ⅛ to 1 inch, but here again this is pure luxury. It is not often that one needs a ⅛-inch chisel. Yet when such a thing is needed, a wider one will not do. On the other hand, when a 1-inch tool is needed, a ½-inch chisel may be substituted.

The all-purpose chisel is known to carpenters and cabinet-makers as a firmer. The firmer chisel is so called because it is thicker and firmer than the thin paring chisel which has a bevelled edge and a longer blade. A third type, used principally in setting butt-type door hinges, is known as a butt chisel. There is no reason, however, why either one of the former types cannot be used for this purpose. More will be said later about the proper use of the chisel.

An experienced man using a chisel may sharpen it by hand but the beginner should use one of the holders that permit the blade of the tool to be held at just the proper angle as it moves over the surface of the oilstone. The angle of the chisel's cutting edge was not determined by accident. It must be preserved in its original form if the tool is to cut properly. Any slight rounding of the actual cutting edge will be fatal, causing the chisel to chew rather than cut. These little sharpening carriages are not expensive, and they are far more than luxuries to beginners. As a parting word on chisels, it may be said that the average worker with wood does not sharpen his chisels nearly as much as they should be sharpened. One is also led to remark that chisels were not made for cutting nails or tin.

There are four main types of planes, the distinction being largely a matter of size. The very long ones (22 to 24 ins.)

are jointer planes, if made of metal, or trying-planes, if made of wood. The 14-17-inch ones are called jack planes, and are used for the rough or heavy work, and the 8—9-inch smoothing planes, usually made of steel. This last tool is used, as its name suggests, for smoothing or finishing the work, after the jack plane has been used.

The very smallest of the planes and a tool usually about 7 inches in length, is called a block plane. These, even when

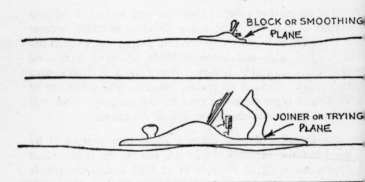

FIGS. 3 and 4. A short plane will cut a wavy surface when called upon to square a long edge, while the long jointer plane will bring square, accurate edges to long boards.

of good quality, are not expensive and are very useful both in smoothing the edges of small pieces and in squaring the ends of boards across the grain. It will be understood, of course, that such a short plane cannot easily be used in accurately smoothing and squaring the edge of a long board. It will cut no doubt but varying pressure applied to the tool as it moves along will cause the blade to cut slight undulations or waves. Here the use of a plane with a long bed or bottom (jointer or trying plane) is indicated, the longer the better if the wavy effect is to be entirely avoided on the long boards (see Figs. 3 and 4).

If the worker cannot afford a whole set of planes, he will find that most of his needs are met by a medium-sized jack plane of good quality. More will be said later about the proper use of planes in squaring, cutting down to size, etc.

The same precautions hold in sharpening plane blades as hold in the case of chisels and more will be said later about this subject.

The jaws of cheap bit braces (see Fig. 5) are soft, the internal threads are badly cut in soft steel, the handles are mounted without bearings and of poorly seasoned wood, etc. That should be enough to warn one away from such costly cheap things.

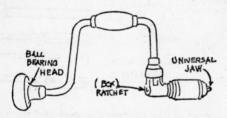

FIG. 5. A brace of good design and construction. Due to universal jaws this tool may be used to hold twist drills with round shanks or bits with square ones. Screwdrivers, countersinks and expansion bits are also made for use with such braces.

Cheap bits, too, are very expensive because they are not worth what one has to pay for them aside from giving poor service, requiring constant sharpening and chewing holes in wood even when sharp.

Perhaps as few as four bits ($\frac{1}{4}$, $\frac{3}{8}$, $\frac{1}{2}$ and 1 inch) will suffice to begin with. Someday maybe the exchequer will bear up under the weight of a whole set of good bits in a box made especially for workshop storage.

An expansion bit (see Fig. 6) may not be needed at first but every home cabinetmaker and carpenter sooner or later has a need for such an instrument. The expansion bit is adjustable through a movable blade and holes up to more than 3 inches in diameter may be cut with it. The minimum hole made is not under 1 inch. These bits usually cost 10s. to 15s. There is no substitute for them unless it is a compass saw, which would be awkward for a hole under 4 inches in diameter. The shank of such bits is similar to the tapered square shank of the ordinary bit and is therefore taken by the chuck on the ordinary brace.

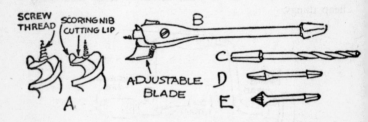

FIG. 6. Two types of bits, one with fine screw and one with coarser screw, are shown at A. At B is an expansion bit adjustable to a diameter of 3 inches. C, an ordinary metal twist drill, D, a screwdriver, and E, a countersink for woodscrew heads, all with square shanks.

While the brace is being equipped with bits, one should not overlook the purchase of a countersink bit. These bore conical shaped counter holes with a taper similar to the woodscrew head so that the head of a woodscrew will set flush.

Another invaluable and inexpensive accessory for the brace is a screwdriver bit. This is simply a screwdriver with a tapered square shank similar to that of a round bit. When used in a bit brace, screws may be driven home speedily and with very little effort.

Where woodscrews are used (and they should replace nails in all good cabinet work involving furniture) it is often advisable to drill either a small starting hole or a hole smaller than the diameter of the screw for the full length of the screw. The latter prevents splitting of the wood. Wood bits do not come in the small sizes needed for this work and therefore carbon drills intended for metal are used. Unfortunately these have round shanks and do not work too well in the chucks of bit braces. Such drills are supplied with square shanks (see Fig. 6), but the low r.p.m. of the brace does not recommend its use with them, especially if one has a large number of screw holes to drill. It is better to purchase a small hand drill or breast drill. In these tools the chuck is driven through a train of two gears and its r.p.m. is sufficiently high to make fast drilling possible.

A set of small twist drills from $\frac{1}{8}$ to $\frac{1}{4}$ inch will suffice. Such a variety will accommodate practically any size woodscrew used in home repair or cabinet repairing.

A small book could be written about saws. In fact the Disston Company has such a booklet which may be had for the asking. The greatest curse in a home shop can be a cheap set of saws unless one wishes to indulge in physical training along with his hobby. The stuff in a saw is of the utmost importance if the tool is going to remain sharp and keep its set. By set is meant the offset of the teeth. This offset, along with sharpness, will be kept for a long time in a good blade. The sharpness can be re-established after long use by the aid of a saw vice, a guide and a three-cornered file. The

B

proper set is given to the teeth by the use of a saw set, a tool resembling a pair of pliers. However, it is not recommended that the beginner make such purchases. Rather, a dull saw should be taken to a local carpenter or other person experienced in such work. After the teeth have been properly set and filed, the saw is just as good as new and the job will last a long time unless one is in the habit of sawing through nails.

In case the home carpenter wishes to go all out with his hobby and desires to learn by experience in restoring saws, the cost of the saw vice, clamp and set is not great. A few pounds will be sufficient to purchase all of the equipment needed. Patience will be required, however, although when a guide is used for filing there will be little reason for failure. Experienced hands can file teeth without the benefit of a filing guide.

A pair of full-size saws will be needed, one a ripsaw, for going down the grain of a long board, and one a crosscut saw, for cutting at right angles to the grain. If the budget is so tight as to prevent such an investment at first, then only the crosscut saw should be bought. This may be used for ripping, the only concession being that of speed in cutting.

One is surprised at the number of special-purpose saws that may be had. Both rips and crosscuts come in small and larger sizes and with what is known as straight and skew-backs, the back of the saw being the top or non-cutting edge. Such saws also come with fine, medium or coarse teeth. The medium type of tooth is most suited to home shop use. The blades of good saws are also ground with a taper to prevent binding and the steel of the blade is such as to avoid holding a bend when the saw binds in cutting wood.

Sooner or later the woodworker will need what is known as a tenon saw as at C in Fig. 7. This is a saw with heavy oblong blade provided with a heavy steel spine on its upper edge so that the blade will not bend during cutting. Such saws are invaluable in cutting off small boards square. Ordinary crosscut saws are started on the edge of a board and held at an angle during the cutting. The edge of the tenon saw is placed on the pencil line of a cut and cutting starts with the saw edge parallel to the surface of the board.

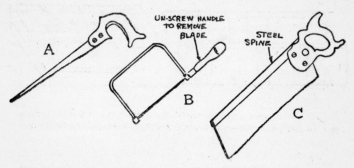

FIG. 7. A compass saw (A). These now come with interchangeable blades of different widths or various radii. (B) A common type of scroll saw for cutting very small radii. (C) A tenon saw used for producing accuracy in cross-grain cutting on small cabinet work. Such saws are also used in mitre boxes for cutting at different angles.

If one wishes, a small wooden mitre box for 45° cuts may be made (as in Fig. 8) for use with a tenon saw.

A manufactured mitre box is a nice thing to have, especially in cabinet work, but a good one is costly. Its purchase may be delayed for a long time.

In the tenon saw class there is also the smaller dovetail saw. This is similar to the ordinary tenon saw save that the blade is narrower and the teeth much finer. Unless one contemplates an early graduation into the class of those who can make good dovetail joints, the purchase of such a tool can be postponed.

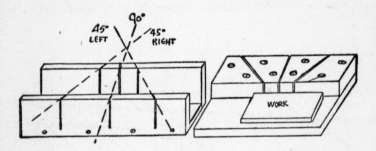

FIG. 8. Two types of home-made mitre boxes for use with a tenon saw in cutting angles as in picture framing, hanging, moulding, etc.

Then there is the so-called keyhole saw, a saw with a long, narrow blade which is used for fret work; certainly not for keyholes except perhaps in the olden days when keys were larger than they are to-day. Such saws are nice to have about but their purchase may be delayed.

Most beginners mistake a compass saw for a keyhole saw. The blade of the compass saw is much wider than that of a keyhole saw and is intended to cut around curves of large radius. Of course, the smaller the radius of a curve the less the width of the saw blade should be. Really, the keyhole saw is the substitute for the power-driven band saw. Sooner or later one will wish to cut curves and therefore the compass saw is recommended for early purchase. In modern form, these saws come with three blades, which may be set into the wooden handle and clamped into position. The smaller blade may be used for cutting around very sharp curves, as sharp as that which could be taken by a band saw.

There is also the veneer saw and the so-called stairbuilder's saw, but these are too highly specialised to be necessary for home shop use.

For fret or scroll work in connection with thin panels of wood, the coping saw is needed. These come with very narrow blades and will take corners too sharp for even the power-driven band saws. Coping saws are not expensive and every shop should have one with a wide assortment of blades. The latter cost only a few pence each. So much for saws (see Fig. 7).

A beginner might pass the matter of screwdrivers off very lightly. That would be a mistake. Many is the fine board that has received a deep and ugly dig from the blade of a cheap or badly chosen screwdriver, the tip of which slipped from the screw slot when heavy pressure was applied. This is a maddening experience. The only insurance against it is a set of good screwdrivers and the use of the right one in the right place. The tip of the screwdriver used should be as wide as the diameter of the screw used and the width of the tip of the screwdriver should be just slightly less than the width of the slot in the screw. Not only that but the edges

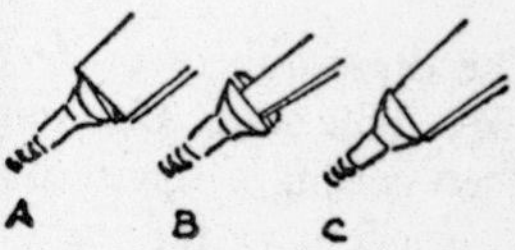

FIG. 9. (A) Screwdriver too large. (B) Screwdriver too small. (C) Screwdriver just right. Blade tip should be square, about the width of slot in screw, and blade should drop to bottom of screw slot.

of the tip of the screwdriver should be ground clean and square if the tool is not to slip during use. Perhaps as many as five screwdrivers of different size should be on hand and they should be good. One may have as many as a dozen of good quality and different sizes without being considered extravagant. See Fig. 9.

A drawknife is often handy to have about a shop although it does not need to be included in the first assortment. Some call drawknives spokeshaves but this is wrong. The drawknife has a naked blade the forged ends of which are bent at right angles to the blade and fitted with drive-on wooden grips or handles. The spokeshave is designed in the manner of a plane with an adjustable blade set in a cast iron frame.

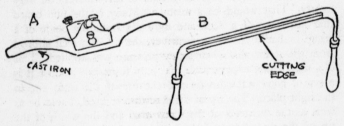

FIG. 10. (A) Spokeshave which operates on principle of plane with adjustable blade. (B) Drawknife usually used for making heavy cuts. It is pulled toward the operator.

The drawknife takes deep heavy cuts while the spokeshave takes light ones. One might start a job with a drawknife, as when cutting a square piece into a round one, and end with the spokeshave for the finishing cuts (see Fig. 10).

Aside from a few other small items like squares (see Figs. 11 and 12), rulers, etc., the foregoing should cover just about

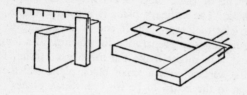

Fig. 11. The ordinary try-square used in all cabinet work and in making small repairs.

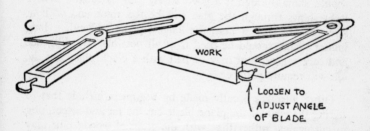

Fig. 12. The " sliding-bevel " which has an adjustable blade but may also be used either as a mitre square or a try-square.

all the beginner will need for his shop. If he learns to use these tools skilfully, he may accomplish any job that can be done with any of the power tools with the exception of the moulding cutter. He may not accomplish his work as quickly, but there is some reason to believe that he will do as well as the man working with power tools and he has a right to claim greater satisfaction and more credit.

It usually happens that the beginning woodworker has an oversimplified viewpoint on all of the common tools. The use of many of these tools is not nearly as simple as one might think. The ordinary plane is a good example. Really it is a tricky tool especially if one is attempting to set up two butting edges in preparation for glueing. If a long board is at hand, one might make the mistake of trying to form such a flat surface with a small block plane which is short in relation to the board to be worked. Such planes produce undulations not visible to the eye save when the planed surface is laid on a true surface and then held up to the light.

When the edges of two boards are being prepared for glueing the boards should always be butted and the joint held between the eye of the worker and a light. No light should show through if a good strong joint is sought. Where light shows through the glue will be too thick and without strength. In such a case, the longest plane at hand, a long jointer plane, should be used if at all possible. By diligence and care a good butt may be had with a block plane but the job will require patience.

Other mistakes usually made by beginners include that of setting the edge of the plane blade out too far and attempting to cut against rather than with the grain of wood. One may take a heavy cut first where a lot of stock is to be removed but as the line is approached the edge of the tool should be set back for a lighter cut. Experience will show that running the finger over the edge of the plane blade will permit one to determine the depth of the cut that will be made.

Even pressure on the plane is also important and if the edge of the tool is to be preserved for the greatest length of time, the plane should be lifted from the work on the *back stroke*.

The perfectly square edge is another problem and it cannot be achieved save by the frequent use of the square, especially when the line is approached. One must also be careful about pressure at the beginning and the end of the cut if a bellying effect is to be avoided. As a plane reaches the end of a board and the front of the plane leaves the board, the trailing knife or blade will cut deeper. Thus one tries to hold the plane perfectly level at this point and to prevent the tip of the tool from dipping downward as it leaves the board. The same in reverse holds for the beginning of the cut. Here the heel of the plane should be prevented from dipping downward. This will cause the blade to cut too deeply also. Thus the board being worked upon will become high in the centre if these precautions are not observed.

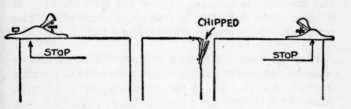

FIG. 13. To square the end of a board, a block plane is used and worked from edge to edge toward the centre. If the cutter of the plane is permitted to pass over the edge of a board in the wrong direction, it will tear off slivers of wood as shown in the centre of above sketch.

As a plane is moved forward over the edge of a board, one should also try to prevent wobbling from side to side. This has a bevelling effect. If the worker frequently runs the eye down the board and makes frequent use of the square such mistakes may usually be avoided. These simple checks may be made without removing a board from a vice.

The block plane is usually used across the end grain of a board when squaring is sought here. Any plane may be used for such work but the block plane is best. Here the beginner is apt to make the mistake of sweeping across the entire end of the board. That will be fatal. As the blade of the plane reaches the far end of a board, it will invariably rip off a chip of wood. Here the craftsman who knows his business always works from each end toward the middle. This bellies out the middle but this belly can be planed off after the ends have been planed (see Fig. 13).

In working on end grain, the craftsman always sets his plane to take away a very thin cut. A thick cut here will produce a tearing action and leave the end of a board ragged and unsightly. In any case, work on end grain should never be done with a dull blade or even a semi-sharp blade. This work calls for the best possible edge on a tool.

Plane knives or cutters may be sharpened in the manner of chisels, the worker making sure that the bevel of the knife is preserved at all costs. A poor bevel will not cut properly. Also nicks in the edges of a blade will leave ridges on a piece of work. Such nicks cannot be ground or taken out of a blade on an oilstone save by long and tedious application. It is best that they be ground out on the side of a small abrasive wheel, the worker being careful to preserve the angle of the blade bevel. He must also be careful not to draw the temper of the blade by overheating. If he does overheat it, the blade will no longer hold its edge for any length of time. The blade is kept cool during grinding by repeated dips into a convenient can of cold water. After grinding the nick out, the blade should be sharpened on an oilstone. If possible a wheel of fine grit should be used to grind out the nick. Naturally the

hole length and breadth of the cutting edge of the blade is
round away uniformly until the nick disappears. To grind
cally near the nick will destroy the contour of the cutting
dge.

One more thing: When the worker sets the blade in the
lane and adjusts the edge for the type of cut to be made, he
ust make sure that the cutting edge of the blade is perfectly
quare with the bottom or sole of the plane. A good cabinet-
aker can determine this quickly by merely running his finger
ver the cutting edge. A better way for the beginner is to
old the bottom of the plane up to his eye level and to run
is eye down the bottom from the front edge. Even a poor
easuring eye will be able to detect a slight maladjustment.
ll planes are provided with facilities for correcting such
accuracies.

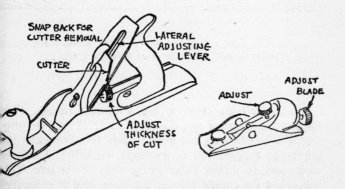

Figs. 14 and 15. A smoothing plane (left) of typical construction
nd of junior jack plane type. What is known as a smoothing plane
ay be from 7 to 10 inches long. A jack plane is about 14 to 18
nches and a jointer plane may be 24 inches long. A block plane
right) is the smallest of the plane family and is used mostly for
mall work or squaring the ends of boards across the grain.

If a plane shows a tendency for the mouth (the slot throug▌ which the cutting edge of the blade protrudes) to foul to▌ frequently with chips, it usually happens that the blade is se▌ too far forward or that one is curling off stock of a thicknes▌ that the mouth of the plane was not made to accommodate▌ When too thick a cut is being made, a plane (even a goo▌ one) has a tendency to rip rather than to cut.

If the worker will follow out these common-sense direction▌ in the use of the plane, he will have little trouble with suc▌ a tool and the finer points of its use will reveal themselve▌ to him as he gains experience (see Figs. 14, 15 and 16).

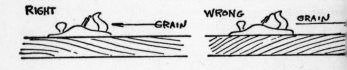

FIG. 16. The right and wrong way to plane across the grain of wood. Planing should always be done with the grain.

The two adjustments on a plane are simple enough. First there is the adjusting nut, directly forward of the rear grip, that lifts the blade up and down. Then directly back of the upper and exposed end of the blade one will find a lever which may be moved either to the right or the left. This will adjust the cutting edge of the blade until it is paralle▌ with the plane bottom (see Fig. 14).

There is also the matter of the universal plane, but this is an expensive tool, coming as it does with blades of many shapes for the cutting of moulding, beading, fluting, etc. The average home workman will not need to use such an▌

nstrument more than once in a blue moon and hence this reatment will stop at the mention of the device.

It may appear almost insulting to some even to mention he use of saws, but few men use them properly. The saw s usually taken for granted just like a hammer. For the noment, reference is made only to the ordinary crosscut saw und the ripsaw. All other types of saw—keyhole, compass, enon saw, etc.—do not come in either rip or crosscut type. Their teeth usually resemble those used on crosscuts.

This may sound trite but a great deal of sawing trouble s caused by rusty saws or saws upon which grease or oil has peen placed and permitted to gum. Oil and fine emery powder is a cure for the former while a petrol-soaked rag will quickly repair the latter. In any case, rust should be prevented either by keeping the saw in an almost air-tight drawer or the saw should be smeared with a light oil between jobs.

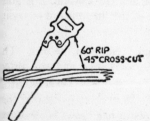

Fig. 17. The proper angles for sawing when using ripsaws or cross-cut saws. Maximum cutting speed is maintained if these angles are used.

The ripsaw is made for cutting with the grain. The teeth have an angle of 8° on the front and 52° on the back. The upper half of each tooth is set, alternately, one to the right, one to the left, to give clearance. This set is equal to one third or less of the thickness of the blade.

The position for ripping should be such as to permit long easy strokes. The user who does most of the cutting with few inches of the blade, in the middle of the saw, has difficult in keeping the line of the cut straight. He also dulls the saw more rapidly because a few teeth are called up to do al the cutting. Full strokes are desirable in both ripping and crosscutting.

In ripping the cut should be started with the finer teeth at the point of the blade. Ripping usually is done with the work supported on sawhorses, but if the board must be held in a vice, it is placed to give the proper cutting angle.

An angle of 60° between the edge of the saw and the face of the work gives the best results when using a rip-saw. Rip saws cut with extreme ease when kept properly sharpened It is not necessary to force them in the cut (see Figs. 17 and 18).

No saw can be expected to give good service indefinitely without resharpening. In ripping and crosscutting, it is good practice to cut on the waste side of the line, instead of trying to halve the line.

Ripsaws are made 5, 5½, 6 and 7 points to the inch. The 5½- and 6-point tools are most widely used and will prove most satisfactory for general work. Some craftsmen, however prefer blades toothed 7 points to the inch.

The length of either rip or crosscut hand saws is measured from point to butt on the cutting edge. Both crosscut and ripsaws are made in various lengths, the 26-inch being the most popular. Crosscut saws are made with blades 20, 22, 2 and 26 inches long; and ripsaws with blades 22, 24 and 2 inches. Saws 24 inches and shorter are known as panel saws The 22-inch, 10-point crosscut is most popular among the shorter saws.

The amount of set given a saw is highly important because it determines the ease with which the saw runs; it ensures accuracy of cutting, and it helps keep the saw sharp for a longer time.

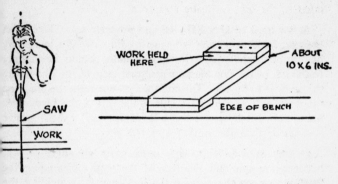

FIG. 18. Greater accuracy in following a layout line will be had if the eye is kept above the saw as illustrated at left. FIG. 19. The bench hook (above) holds small work when the tenon saw is used for cutting across grain.

The nature and character of the wood to be cut must be considered also. Green or wet wood requires a saw with coarse teeth and wide set, 6 or 7 points to the inch, while a 10- or 11-point saw with light set will work better in dry, well seasoned timber. For ordinary crosscutting, the user will find the 7-, 8- or 9-point most in demand.

Points to the inch is a term used to designate the size of teeth in a saw. The saw with a small number of tooth points to the inch, 6 or 7 for example, will make a rough cut, yet cut fast. Saws with more points, say 10 or 11 points, will make smooth even cuts.

The crosscut saw, being designed to cut across the grain, cuts with an action similar to a number of small knife blades. The front face of the teeth of a crosscut saw have an angle of 15°, the back of the teeth have an angle of 45°. The teeth are usually filed with a bevel of about 24°. The upper half of each tooth is set, alternately, one to the right, the other to the left, to insure clearance.

A saw must be kept SHARP and properly set. The correct position for crosscutting is shown in Fig. 18. An imaginary line through the saw, arm and shoulder would be slightly to the left of the saw blade, permitting view of the line where the work is to be cut. To start the cut, one rests the blade on the waste side of the line, supports the side of the blade with the thumb and draws the saw a few times until a slight groove is formed; then the worker cuts straight with a full stroke.

In crosscutting, it is best to maintain an angle of 45° between the saw and the face of the work. Extending the forefinger along the side of the handle aids in guiding the blade. One takes long, easy strokes and makes each stroke do its work.

Supporting the waste side of the work with one hand will prevent the wood from splintering on the under side when the cut is nearly completed.

The worker looks carefully at repair work to see that there are no nails in the path of saw. Good craftsmen do not throw saws around. Blades are covered with a thin coat of light oil and hung up when not in use.

When ripping, amateurs often run off the line. In such a case, the saw can easily be brought back to follow the line if the cutting is for a moment done with the first few inches (near the tip) and the saw blade bent or twisted at the same time and in the proper direction.

There is little that can be said about a tenon saw except that if possible a craftsman should have one and it should be about 10 inches long and with 15 points (number of teeth to inch).

The tenon saw is simply used for small accurate cuts. Not only is the blade of the saw thick but a steel spine runs along the top edge of the blade and this prevents the saw bending or squirming during a cut. The use of a simple bench hook (see Fig. 19) will be very handy with such a tool.

If the amateur woodworker wishes, he may make a very simple substitute for a mitre box as illustrated in Fig. 8. While three slots or saw guides are shown (90°, 45° left, 45° right) there is no reason why more cannot be cut as they are needed or when the gadget is made.

If a man understands the operation of a tool the chances are that he will be better able to use that tool intelligently. Too many tyros think the ordinary auger bit a complete mystery. Perhaps another glance at Fig. 6 will dispel the mystery of the auger bit. The names of the various parts are here given. The operation of the tool is as follows: At the top of the tool is an ordinary wood screw thread. When this is placed on a piece of wood and turned under pressure, the screw thread enters the wood pulling the cutting portion of the bit after it.

Next part to reach the surface of the wood after the screw has entered are the two side projections called the scoring nibs. These cut into the wood leaving deep circular scoring, followed by the cutting lips which peel off circular shavings. For efficient work, it is essential that the nibs be sharp, the threads of the screw be without damage, especially the point, and that the cutting lips be sharp.

There are different types of bits, too, some of them with different fluting. What the worker wishes to know, however, is whether he should purchase his set of bits single thread screw point (see Fig. 6) or double. The answer is that double is best for fine work.

C

Often does the beginning woodworker ask, "How is it that one cuts a clean hole with a brace and bit?" It usually happens that as the bit protrudes from the opposite side of the work, it bursts through, tearing off a number of along-grain chips with it. Such accidents may be prevented in two ways. In the one case the bit is withdrawn just before it breaks through on the opposite side of a board. This should be done just as the tip of the bit screw breaks through. Then boring is started from the opposite side, placing the tip of the screw in the hole already made. This latter cutting is done gently and it will usually be found that the nibs will cut sufficiently deep to remove the circle of wood left.

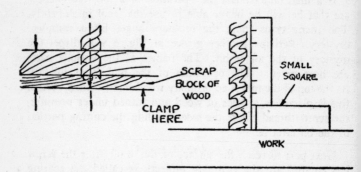

FIG. 20. By clamping a piece of scrap wood to a board (left), damage is prevented as a bit goes through. FIG. 21. Use of try-square helps keep bit vertical during boring.

The cleanest method of preventing break-through damage is shown in Fig. 20 where a scrap block of wood is clamped to the back-side of a board to be bored and in such a position that the bit will keep on boring into it after it has pierced the board being worked upon. This leaves a clean hole with clean edges. When boring such a hole in a piece of furniture or other article not available to a bench vice, ordinary wood clamps may be used.

An arrangement such as that in Fig. 21 will help a beginner to bore a hole straight if a deep bore is to be made.

Splitting is usually prevented either by holding work in a vice where the pressure of the jaws is exerted to keep the wood pressed together in a direction at right angles to that in which the hole is being bored, or by the use of wood clamps, a series of them placed near the position of the proposed hole.

Nowadays it is also possible to purchase ordinary twist drills (as intended for drilling holes in metal) with square shanks (see Fig. 6) that will fit a brace. These drills may be very successfully used on wood and it may be advisable to have ¼-inch and ½-inch sizes at hand. The tendency of the ordinary spur or screw bit to split the piece of wood is very great while there is no tendency toward splitting when the metal type of twist drill is employed.

While seldom needed in making furniture repairs, the expansion bit is a handy thing to have about a house (see Fig. 6). Such bits are provided with an adjustable blade bearing a scale which will permit the user to pre-determine the diameter of the hole to be made.

The wood chisel, save in making mortise joints, is not a tool that is often used by the home craftsman. However, a few sharp chisels at hand can be very helpful. These tools are not always used with a mallet. A keen tool can be used to shave off thin chips in awkward corners where neither the plane nor the jackknife can be made to reach. Here the craftsman simply strikes the top of the chisel handle with the heel of his hand. Such an operation is especially effective in cutting across grain in tight quarters.

Again the amateur is warned to keep chisels sharp. A few occasional strokes on a nearby stone will ensure clean cutting and accurate work.

As will be seen by Fig. 22, there are a number of ways in which a hole might be cut for a mortise joint or other purpose. Some craftsmen prefer first to bore out the stock enclosed

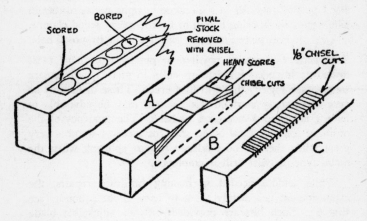

FIG. 22. Sketch A shows how stock is removed with a bit before chiselling. B and C show other methods of cutting a mortise with a chisel.

by the marking, and then remove the remaining stock with a sharp chisel. So far as the amateur is concerned, this is perhaps the easiest method. In any event, the area from which the stock is to be removed is always deeply scored first with the chisel and this scoring is continued at regular intervals all the way through and as stock is removed. Inasmuch as little more than $\frac{1}{8}$ of an inch can be removed at a time, the chisel is used for scoring after each cut of this depth. If the sides and ends of a hole being cut are not kept scored, the wood will be torn away and the side walls, upon completion, will be so rough as to make subsequent glueing of no avail. In all scoring operations, the flat side, as distinguished from the bevelled edge of the tool, should always be kept facing the outside of the enclosed area being worked upon.

Inasmuch as those who refinish cabinet work must sooner or later be introduced to the scraper, this would appear to be the logical spot in which to dispense information concerning this important tool.

Scrapers come in a number of different forms and are supplied in two general types. One is called a cabinet scraper and the other is intended for use in the removal (dry) of old paint and varnish. The latter type is very dangerous in the hands of inexperienced workmen.

FRENCH SWAN NECK STRAIGHT

FIG. 23. At left, the proper method of holding a cabinet scraper. Also illustrated are three types of scrapers supplied to the trade.

The cabinet scraper is supplied in the form of a piece of sheet saw steel and may be had in the shapes shown in Fig. 23. If the shop owner can afford it, a set of three scrapers is recommended. Although very simple, the cabinet scraper is not as easy to manipulate as one might suspect. The proper position is shown in Fig. 23.

This tool is intended to replace or follow the use of the plane in fine cabinet work or it sometimes finds use in positions where the plane cannot be accommodated. The scraper, when sharp, will curl off very thin shavings and leave an excellent surface in its wake. Especially is the use of the cabinet scraper to be sought for employment on veneers for pre-varnishing treatment or for the levelling off of butt joints.

In use, the scraper may be either pushed or pulled. When pushed, the scraper is held firmly in both hands, the fingers on the forward and the thumbs on the back side. It is tilted forward, away from the operator, far enough to prevent chattering. When pulled, the angle of the blade is reversed.

A mistaken idea prevails that scrapers should remove only fine dust. If properly sharpened and skilfully operated they will actually plane.

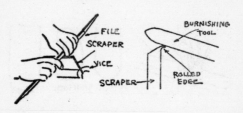

FIG. 24. How a file and burnishing tool are used to sharpen the edges of cabinet scrapers.

The cabinet scraper may be sharpened in two ways—one for ordinary scraping and one for fast scraping. The ordinary method is practised by first placing the scraper in a vice and using a smooth cutting file on all four edges (all edges of a scraper may be used). By draw filing, the worker seeks to set up an edge that is as perfectly square as possible. This done, the smooth-cut file is run backward to dress up the edge. After this, the slight burr left on all four edges of the scraper by the file is ground off by rubbing the scraper on a grinding stone, the scraper being held flat.

In the second method of sharpening a scraper where it is intended to produce a faster cutting edge, each edge, or as many as the worker wishes, is filed to a 30° bevel. Then the cutting edge of the scraper is deliberately given a heavy burr by the use of a burnisher, which is nothing more than a small rod of extra hard steel with a wooden handle used to turn the edge of the bevel in the manner illustrated in Fig. 24.

In use, this turned edge is turned toward the workman and the tool is also drawn toward him.

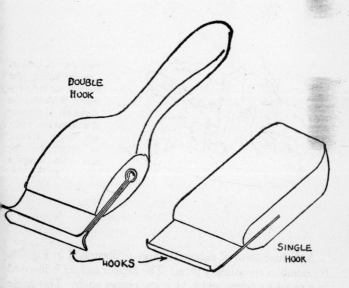

FIG. 25. Types of scrapers used in removing old paint and varnish in dry form. They are also useful in removing remainders after a semi-dry state is reached following use of varnish removers.

Scrapers intended for paint and varnish removers are faster cutting. Other types are shown in Fig. 25. Such scrapers must be kept very sharp and this may be done on a fine-grit grinding wheel.

These latter tools may be treacherous in the hands of a beginner, their sharp edges digging in deeply unless great care is taken. Such blades cut far too fast to be used in the last scraping of a fine piece of cabinet work or cabinet refinishing. Indeed this tool offers so much hazard that no home craftsman should trust himself with it in removing paint or varnish until he has employed it on practice surfaces. In any event, the use of a good paint and varnish remover is to be preferred if one can afford it.

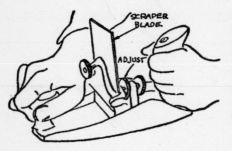

FIG. 26. A cabinet scraper taking the form of an ordinary plane. With this the workman is assured of an even cut, without finger fatigue as might be the case with scrapers used as in Fig. 23.

A de luxe form of cabinet scraper is illustrated in Fig. 26. It resembles an ordinary plane. The cabinet scraper is inserted in a cast-iron frame and held at the proper angle. This angle can be adjusted within narrow limits by the screws shown to the back of the blade.

Although not essential to a tool kit, the marking gauge shown in Fig. 27 is most convenient to use when a great deal

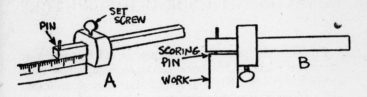

FIG. 27. Marking gauge. The gauge is set with a ruler as shown (A), and the marking is done with scoring pin as sketched (B).

of mortising is being done. Such gauges are inexpensive and easily used as will be seen by the drawing. The scoring pin takes the place of a pencil.

FIG. 28. A small, inexpensive hand drill is used in drilling holes for woodscrews.

Where a workman uses many woodscrews, as the repairer of either old or new furniture should, a small hand drill such as shown in Fig. 28 is a necessity. A hole of the proper size should precede the driving of any woodscrew beyond $\frac{1}{2}$ or $\frac{3}{4}$ inch in length.

NEW STRENGTH FOR OLD FURNITURE

There are few repairs to either new or old furniture that cannot be made in the home workshop with a few well-chosen hand tools. Indeed a clever worker may often furnish his home with excellent furniture purchased in secondhand shops and repaired and refinished. In one case, the author heard of an enterprising young man who purchased his furniture at less than cost price from a large furniture store because of damage certain pieces suffered during transit.

One fault of the average would-be repairer of furniture is haste; not only in execution but also in contemplation. It rarely happens that there is more than one good way to repair a piece of furniture and it well pays the beginner to come as close to that one best way as possible. Each job must be studied carefully before work is begun if a satisfactory and lasting repair is to be made.

There are two articles of furniture that require special attention because they are called upon to bear up under heavy strain. In the one case there are things in the category of chairs, sofas, etc. In the second case there are tables and stands where the long leverage of legs make repairs to them of great importance if the repairs are to last. Chairs will be treated first.

At the outset let it be said that there are precious few repairs on chairs than can be made with the aid of glues, nails or cements alone. No glue is that good and nails should never be used for the simple reason that all chairs worth repairing are made of the harder woods through which nails are driven with difficulty and the danger of splitting. Drill a hole through the wood before the nail is driven? A mere makeshift! Nails driven in this manner never hold well.

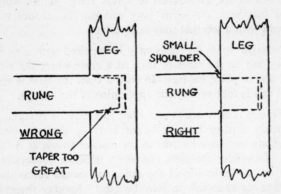

FIG. 29. Taper on the chair rung at left is far too great. Rather than a taper, a newly installed chair rung should have a small shoulder and a close or drive fit.

As a simple and common repair, one might mention loose rungs (called stretchers). A quick smear of even the best glue is not going to make a lasting repair. The rung or rails in modern or semi-modern chairs usually come loose due to wood shrinkage which results in a bad fit. Bad fits are never repaired by a copious application of glue or cement. To be effective, glue must be applied thinly and subjected to great pressure while setting up. Thick bodies of glue are brittle and without strength.

Of course, it often happens that the best repair for a broken rung is a new one. If the chair is a painted one and the worry of producing a match of wood colour is not present, then the worker may simply purchase a maple dowel of the right size at the local timber yard, cut it to length and insert it, making sure that a tight fit is had and that a good grade of glue is applied. Here glue is important because the fit is tight.

The drawing (Fig. 29) shows the simple mistake to be avoided in the installation of a new rung. If the workman will fuss with the joints long enough, his labours will be repaid with a job that may outlive him.

Straight splits on rungs may be repaired with glue if the rungs are on the sides or back of a chair where the sitter is not apt to place his feet. In such a case, the glue is applied and this is followed by the application of the clamps.

Square rails or rungs and chair legs may be repaired more securely if they have sufficient body so that the cleat or mending iron may be used in the manner shown at A in Fig. 30. To render the cleat absolutely invisible (naturally it is put on the underside of the rail), one should recess the rail so that the cleat will fit into the wood. Another thing: holes should be drilled for the woodscrews if splitting is to be prevented. Also nothing will be harmed by smearing the joint with glue before the cleat is finally screwed into position. The joint might be pulled up tight enough to make the glue effective.

Oftentimes in making repairs to chairs, the use of a tourniquet is advised. Rope is never to be recommended for this purpose because no matter how tight it is pulled up at first, it will stretch and loosen under continued strain. It is better to use wire and protect the wood or finish of the chair by placing thick soft pads of cloth under the wire before the tourniquet is pulled up tight. Twenty-four hours should be allowed for the setting of the glue.

Where no strain is to be involved and where the screw heads will be hidden, it is possible to use the simple repair shown at B in Fig. 30. Here also glue is recommended.

At C in Fig. 30 will be noticed a very effective repair for a shrunken rung end. If a careful fit is made with the wedge and a good grade of glue is applied, this repair will last a long time. One takes care that the wedge does not have too acute a taper and that its blunt end does not protrude too far. The segment to receive the wedge may be cut from the rung end by a fine-bladed saw. This will make for accuracy. One also takes care to see that the end of the wedge has some distance to travel forward before it reaches the end of the cut in the rung.

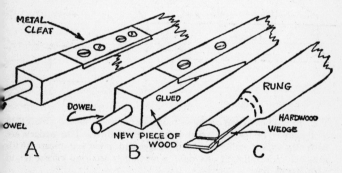

FIG. 30. As at A above, square rungs or stretchers in chairs should be held in place with glued dowels and repairs may be made as at A or B. C shows how a round rung may be notched out to receive a thin wedge which is driven in when the rung is forced into the socket and which expands the end of the rung. The wedge and rung are smeared with glue before installation.

As the rung end moves into the socket in the leg of the chair, it will be seen that the wedge will be driven deeper into the tapered cut made in the end of the rung. This will have the effect of spreading the rung end inside the socket.

In the case of loose joints in chairs with square rails, one is apt to find mortise and tenon joints as illustrated in Fig. 31. Here the wedge treatment as used with round rungs may also be applied along with dowels if the case is a bad one. In case one or two ¼-inch dowels are used, they should be driven in from the inside face of the chair leg where these ends will be less noticed.

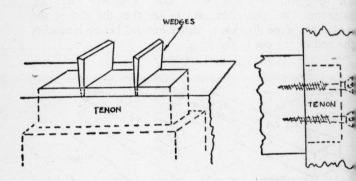

FIG. 31. When repairing loose mortise and tenon joints, small, thin wedges may be used to expand the tenon slightly. The wedges are driven in with a mallet and both wedges and tenon are smeared with glue before installation. At right, a method of securing a loose tenon with woodscrews.

In speaking of dowels, it is recommended that one purchase the spirally-grooved dowels if possible. Such a dowel costs a bit more than the smooth surface dowel but it does a better job in carrying along glue to the interior of a dowel hole.

The repair of chair legs will call forth all of the skill of the average amateur craftsman. Anything called upon to withstand weight and to resist squirming and twisting at the same time calls for skill.

If one is called in to do a bit of major surgery on a chair with large square legs, the chances are that the job can be done with very little trouble. On the other hand, when a slight round leg is broken or split, then real trouble is ahead.

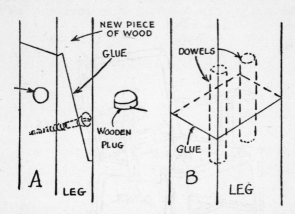

FIG. 32. At **A** is shown a method of repairing a square chair leg. The holes for the screws are counter bored (not countersunk) and a small wooden plug is inserted. A butted dowel repair is shown at **B**.

Fig. 32 will take care of the ways in which to repair broken square legs. The neatest and most workmanlike job is shown at A. If the two pieces are carefully fitted and glued before either the screws or the dowels are driven home, then a fine, strong, job cannot help but result. Naturally small clamps should be applied to this joint while the glue is setting up.

The front legs of chairs are usually jointed into the front corners of the frame with mortise and tenon, or dowels. In really good chairs (see Fig. 33), such joints are usually reinforced with corner blocks. In any event, the joints, no matter how well made, especially in the case of modern chairs, are very apt to come loose either through excessive abuse or through shrinkage due to poor seasoning of the wood or no seasoning at all. In the latter case, the joint may become excessively loose and require a major repair.

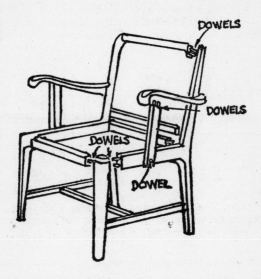

FIG. 33. The method used in producing a factory-made chair of the present time. This does not depart a great deal from the method employed a hundred years ago.

Perhaps one of the most effective repairs in such a case is the use of shims. A shim simply amounts to a thin piece of open grained wood carefully glued to one face of the joint as shown in Fig. 34. This is done only after the old glue has been carefully removed, with a piece of sandpaper on a block of wood, to ensure leaving as flat a surface as possible. The shim is glued in place and left under the pressure of clamps at least all night. The shim should be much thicker than needed so that it may be cut down with a block plane and then sanded to a semi-drive fit before the joint is finally glued together.

Wedges may also be applied in the manner illustrated in Fig. 31, but this is a more difficult job than the installation of a shim and has no advantage over the shim method of treatment.

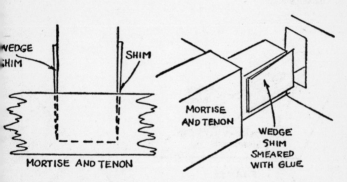

FIG. 34. Another method of using thin, wedge-like shims in repairing loose mortise and tenon joint.

It is not usual that one finds a leg so installed in a chair frame that the installation of a corner block will not be of any aid in so far as the leg itself is concerned, although great and good service may be done to the chair frame in general. For the latter purpose the corner block is almost a panacea. But there are corner blocks *and* corner blocks. A jerry-made corner block of 1-inch soft pine cut with a loose fit and installed with the wrong kind of screws, or with nails, amounts to a waste of time.

To serve their purpose effectively, corner blocks should be

D

as large as possible, at least $1\frac{1}{2}$ inches thick, and cut from birch or some similar hardwood. The fit of the block into the corner of a chair frame, or into the corner of any article of furniture for that matter, is of the greatest importance. What we seek here, above all else, is flat surfaces coming together with as large a contact area as possible. Thus one may fuss for a long time bringing this about, but it will not be time lost for the resulting joint will be that much better, especially if glue is applied before the corner block is screwed into place.

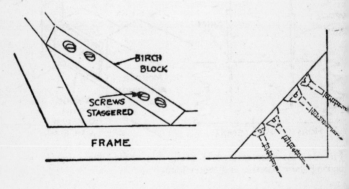

Figs. 35 and 36. The faithful and not-to-be-beaten corner block installed with glue and woodscrews (left). Corner blocks should be as large and as thick as possible and of hard wood, with plenty of opportunity for the holding screws to engage both the block and the article repaired (right). Clearance holes for screws are drilled through the block, which must be carefully fitted to its corner.

The number and type of screws used and the method of their placement is also important. It depends upon the size of the block whether two or four screws must be used. For best results, clearance holes for the screws are first drilled through the block and these are countersunk for the screw heads. Figs. 35 and 36 will show good technique in such a repair. It is noted here that all four screws pass through the main body of the block and that they are not too near the corner of the block where the wood stock lacks body.

Some mechanics prefer to use some of the wrought iron mending irons such as those illustrated in Fig. 37.

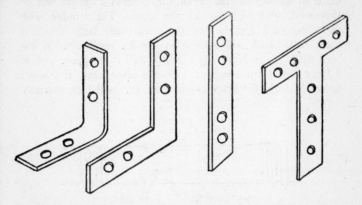

FIG. 37. Mending irons may be purchased at the ironmonger's in different shapes and sizes.

Cleats of this sort, obtainable in various sizes from local ironmongers, are very useful but the writer for one is not given to the use of the angles as substitutes for the wooden corner blocks. The latter when well-fitted are worth at least three angles. All such angles have a certain " spring " and while they may hold a chair together for a long time, they do not prevent a certain amount of what one may call " give."

In so far as chairs are concerned, the matter of the broken small round leg has been left until last. Here is a job calling for real skill. Wherever possible, and in cases where the leg is simply round and straight, the easiest repair is that of making a whole new leg, giving it what taper it needs with a drawknife, block plane and sandpaper. Oftentimes such a leg may be made from a $1\frac{1}{2}$-inch dowel in maple. These usually come pretty well seasoned.

Another type of repair much more difficult to make than a whole new leg is shown in Fig. 38. No attempt should be made to smooth out the break line, otherwise the leg will be shortened, and will not fit the chair. The trouble with dowelling such legs is that if a sufficiently large dowel is used, little stock will remain in the leg itself after it has been drilled out. Naturally a $\frac{1}{8}$-inch wall is not going to give a large dowel much support. On the other hand, if a small dowel ($\frac{1}{4}$-inch, for instance) is used, this will lack strength.

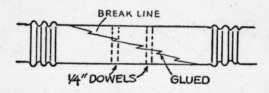

Fig. 38. A glued and dowelled joint in a small round leg for a chair of the fancy Hitchcock type.

Therefore if a home craftsman does provide such a repair on one of his wife's treasured chairs (antiques are the most likely category in which to find delicate chairs with round curved legs), he had best warn her to hide it away when fat Uncle George plans to make a visit.

Much of the cheaper furniture reaches the market to-day with small oblong corner blocks installed as illustrated in Fig. 39. If the writer had attempted such shoddy construction in his manual training class back in 1910, his instructor would have rapped his knuckles and with good excuse. To-day, due to the infantile belief of some manufacturers in the overrated tenacity of certain modern adhesives, cheap furniture reaches the market held together principally by such blocks simply stuck into place without benefit of woodscrews. The writer does not scream out against the use of small corner blocks of this sort, but he does object to their employment when not accompanied by the use of woodscrews along with the adhesive. One reason for the lack of screws on many cheap modern pieces is the fact that screws do not hold well in $\frac{3}{16}$-inch plywood!

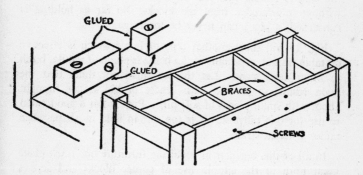

FIGS. 39 and 40. Sketch at left shows how small corner blocks are installed with glue and woodscrews. At right, cross braces installed on table frames along with corner blocks will make an old table as strong as the day it was built.

The home repairer of furniture may often make excellent use of corner blocks of this nature, using them with both screws and a good grade of glue or other adhesive material. Such things work wonders where strength is to be added, especially where flat surfaces at right angles to each other come together. Thus in the case of a commode or chest, the worker might find it desirable to run such an elongated corner piece down each corner and the woodscrews driven in at a 90° angle to each other. The block should also be of hard wood and clearance holes are drilled for the woodscrews. Countersinking is also advisable. This is not done merely to hide the head of the screw but to make most effective use of the shank of the screw where most of its strength lies.

In any case, the corner block should be as large, within reason, as the space in which it is to be installed will allow. The larger it is the more strength it will have. However, in designing such blocks for articles of furniture having drawers, the worker should see to it that the latter are able to close without interference from the blocks. So far as holding is concerned, a block can never be too large.

Fig. 40 will show another type of brace which is effective on table frames, especially if the brace is made of maple, birch or other hard wood. Let the workman not think that the good results to be had with braces or blocks are brought about with small pieces of soft pine. Pine is not a good wood to use for this purpose. It is too soft to hold its shape when under constant strain.

In all of this business of repairing furniture one must place great faith in the simple use of corner blocks and screws wherever such blocks may be used and where they will be completely out of sight.

The dowel is the second best bet and one uses the largest possible size for any job at hand, so long as the stock into which the dowel is driven is stout enough.

Here and there one might find occasion to use the type of mortise and tenon joint illustrated in Fig. 41.

This type proved a life-saver to the author at one time. In this case, he came upon an antique in which the joint had been repaired so many times with nails that the tongue of the mortise and tenon joint was split into ribbons, and had to be sawn off. The previous repairman, whoever he was, thought that box nails were good substitutes for dowels. There is no doubt about their working faster!

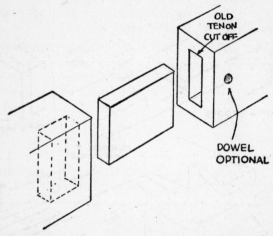

FIG. 41. Where a tenon has been split by driving nails into it, it may be cut off and the position provided with a mortise. A splined tenon may then be installed as illustrated. Dowelling and glueing will help to hold it for a long time.

Although there is no space to go into the making of all the types of joints (see Fig. 42 for illustrations of others) it will be advisable to supply data on the cutting of a simple mortise and tenon.

At the outset let it be known that accuracy is the prime consideration and that this cannot be achieved with haste unless one is experienced in the matter of making such joints.

A loose mortise and tenon is worthless.

To obtain the accuracy that ensures a tight fit, the worker lays the joint out carefully and then, when he removes the majority of the stock, proceeds slowly trying the joint occasionally and being guided accordingly.

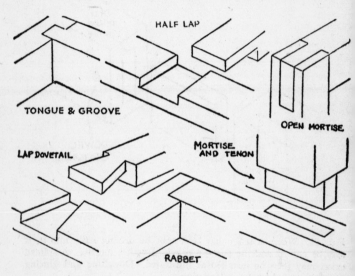

FIG. 42. These joints are commonly met with in old and new furniture.

It is probably best to cut the hole first. The wider the chisel that can be used, the better. In designing such joints it is well to make them just the width of a chisel, say ½ inch, ¾ inch, or 1 inch across. Then at least on two sides of the hole to be cut the worker can proceed without moving his chisel along. In any event, after the hole has been carefully laid out with a sharp pencil, the worker scores the lines deeply with his chisel and mallet. Then he is ready to remove waste.

Let him make very sure that his chisel is just as sharp as he can make it, and let him have his stone at his elbow to give the chisel a few strokes occasionally, especially while he is cutting across grain. Of course in making these cross-grain cuts, the average worker is so impatient as to attempt to cut too deeply before the chips are removed. This can result in a degree of chewing regardless of the sharpness of the chisels used.

In cutting joints either with the saw or with the chisel, the worker simply wishes to make sure that if he is to err, he errs on the right side—by holes being too small rather than too large. One can always cut a hole larger or a tongue smaller, but it is rather difficult to work in the opposite direction.

In the restoration of chests it will usually be found that the drawers fail to function properly, either binding or failing to open altogether. In the case of very old chests where well-seasoned wood was used in construction, the fault is apt to be found in badly worn rails (upon which the drawer slides) or slides at the bottom of the sides of the drawers. In some old chests, many of these members will be found to be worn so badly that the drawer front will no longer remain flush with the front of the chest or the top rail. Rather the drawer will tilt backward because most of such wear is on the back of the rails and drawer slides. Sometimes as much as $\frac{1}{2}$ inch, $\frac{1}{4}$ inch on each member, will be found to be worn away.

Such repairs are quickly and simply made by the aid of a saw, a block plane and a bit of glue. Two thin wedge-shaped or slightly tapered strips are cut and glued to the position shown in Fig. 43. These should be over-size in thickness so that the block plane may be used to cut them down during the fitting. Brads are not recommended for use with the glue because of the planing to size after the glue has dried.

Rather than going to the trouble of building up to the worn rails inside the chest, it is best to use oversize repairs on the drawers themselves. This will compensate for the wear on the rails.

The drawers of older chests are also found in a generally weakened condition and unable to hold their shape due to the failure of the dovetailed joints holding the sides to the front and back pieces.

So far as repairs to badly damaged dovetails go, there is very little to be done about it. Certainly squirting the loose joints full of model aeroplane cement or glue is not going to help matters, although illusionary relief of a temporary nature might be had.

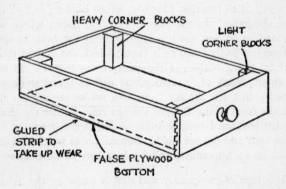

FIG. 43. Ways to strengthen an old chest drawer and to take up wear on the runners. A new false bottom of quarter-inch plywood can be glued over the old bottom and nailed with brads from the sides and ends, or corner blocks can be installed. Both can be used in bad cases. When installing the plywood, the drawer should be perfectly squared and the plywood cut accurately to fit.

In such a case, the workman may use either one of the two methods illustrated in Fig. 43. In one case the good old reliable corner block is used in one or all of the corners, glue only being preferred for its installation. In the other case, a thick false bottom is placed over the old bottom and the two sides and back screwed to it in the manner illustrated. This is usually sufficient to strengthen the front panel. This false bottom should be perfectly square before being set in place and it should also have as good a fit as possible. Smearing the false bottom with a good grade of glue or other adhesive before it is put in place and leaving it clamped to the old bottom for twenty-four hours will help matters a great deal. A good repair of this kind will last for many years.

The refitting of a drawer may proceed from this point. If the drawer binds, it is usually in one or two spots. Smearing the drawer sides with blue carpenter's chalk will help to discover the tight spot. Where the chalk is removed, exposing clean wood, will indicate high spots that need treatment with a block plane. In all cases, the workman proceeds slowly, always keeping in mind that too little is in this case far better than too much.

There is an important point to keep in mind in repairing binding drawers. If, for instance, a chest is moved from a damp spot where it has been for months or years (a cellar for instance where many farmers placed old chests) into a warm dry room, one should allow time for it to dry out before going to work on it. It may be that the binding of the drawers will correct itself in a few weeks. If, then, some heavy planing and refitting of the drawers was indulged in prematurely, a complete drying out of the old chest will find the drawers loose and sloppy. It is better to leave such chests about in their new environment for awhile until they have a chance to condition themselves to it.

The trouble with most modern chests of the cheaper variety

is that they were usually made out of poorly seasoned wood, and very bad design and manufacturing methods brought them into precarious being. Such things are wholly machine-made and they reflect very little credit on their makers. One cannot help lament the crime of permitting some manufacturers to use up our national resources by converting perfectly good forest land into mass-produced junk.

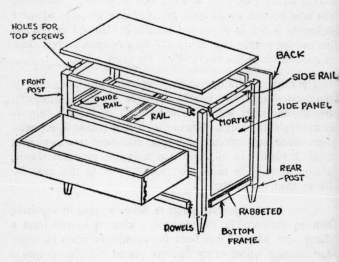

Fig. 44. The method used to construct chests of drawers. The method to-day varies little from that used in the furniture factories of the 1850s.

Many such modern chests also suffer from what might be called general debilitation; everything is wrong with them. However, in contemplating restoration of such pieces, the amateur must learn never to underestimate the curative powers of glue, screws, corner blocks, etc.

Does the chest wobble badly? How about the backboards? Are they split and have the nails come out? If so, one will be surprised at the improvement that will be brought about by removing the old backboards entirely, the good ones with the bad ones, and replacing them with a single piece of ¼-inch or ⅜-inch plywood cut square. If the construction of the chest permits it, this new plywood back should be put in place with screws. Properly installed, such a back should take out 90 per cent of the lateral wobble of any chest.

Wobble in the other direction may come from side panels becoming split or unglued and the loosening of the joints holding the bottom side stretchers (see Fig. 44).

One of the best methods of bracing and strengthening a chest sidewise is shown in Fig. 45. What might be called inside bracing panels are installed, one on each side of the top drawer and one on each side of the bottom drawer. For the sake of clearness, the part of the chest illustrated in Fig. 45 is shown without the top.

The bracing panels are merely oblong pieces of a thick plank fastened to the front and rear posts of the chest by means of woodscrews. To be effective these panels should be of some hard wood like maple and about 1¼ to 1½ inches thick. Also the panels should fit accurately and squarely between the front and rear posts, a mild pressed fit being best. Then, when the four holding screws are installed, an effective brace will be had. Four such braces, properly installed, will be of great assistance in eliminating the wobble of any chest.

If the top and bottom rails on the front of the chest are loose and the joints broken, it will usually be found that such rails are held in place with dowels and that these should be replaced with slightly larger dowels. It will also be possible in most cases to install a carefully fitted corner block here, one that will not only engage the rails but the front posts and side rails as well.

Is the top warped? If it is warped too badly and can be replaced with little trouble, that is the thing to do. In any event, taking the warp out is not merely a matter of clamping the top down and driving in a few screws. If the top is badly warped, clamping it down in a dry condition may split it in a number of places and render it unfit for further use.

Of course, all chest tops may very easily be removed, being screwed into place by screws of the right length coming up

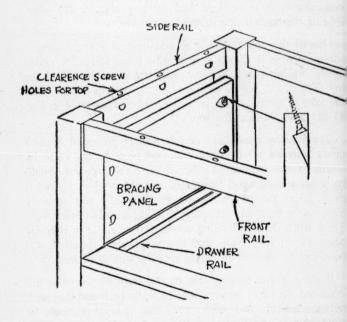

FIG. 45. Heavy slabs of hard wood installed between the front and back posts of a chest of drawers as shown will greatly increase strength. The slab should be as thick as possible. Four slabs are usually enough, two at each end of the chest.

through the top and side rails. The sectionalised drawing previously referred to in Fig. 44 will show this.

Normal warping of a slight nature will usually be remedied by drawing up the old screws. If the threads in the wood are stripped from too many attempts to draw the holding down screws up tighter, then the old holes are plugged with sharpened stick ends and the ends broken off inside the holes. The screws are then replaced. In exceptional cases, it may be necessary, once the top is removed, to drill a few more holes through the end and front top rail and install more screws.

Excessive warping cannot be so easily removed, some of it never. For one thing, excessive warping cannot be conquered by the mere exercise of brute force. Forcing a board back into shape can be done easily enough with clamps but immediately the clamps are removed the board will tend to assume its original contour if it does not split badly in the meantime. Of course with table and chest tops where holding down screws come up through the bottom into the top boards, it may be that once the warp is taken from a board, these screws will keep the warp from returning. It may be that to do this the worker will have to install more screws than were originally used.

Very bad warps are incurable when the grain of the wood is involved in a certain way due to the cutting of the log from which the wood came. Forcing such boards back into shape, even after the precaution of wetting or steaming them, is apt to split them. If a table leaf is involved, the board will in all probability return to its original form after it has dried out. If it does not split in the straightening process, one may prevent this return by the installation of cleats on the back of the table leaf. This is an awkward and unsightly repair but there may be no other answer in the preservation, for instance, of an old family heirloom as close to its original condition as possible. The trouble is that the old cabinetmakers, thorough in every other respect, rarely finished or closed the grain on the back of table leaves or table tops (see Fig. 46).

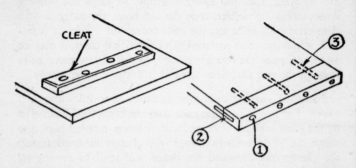

FIG. 46. Two methods of using cleats to prevent mild warps from returning to table leaves. The end cleat shown at the right may be held in place by (1) screws, (2) splines, or (3) dowels. The repair shown at the right is by far the most workmanlike.

Slight warp may be cured by wetting the concave side of a board with hot water and exposing the convex side to gentle heat from the sun or other sources for several hours. Sometimes such restoration will last and sometimes it will not. It depends upon the wood. In any event it will last if the board is used as a table top or chest top where holding down screws are employed from beneath. In such cases, it might be advisable to employ a few more screws, making sure that the new screws are no longer than the old ones (see Fig. 48).

A very badly warped table leaf may be taken to a timber-yard and treated in the manner shown in Fig. 47. The board is first sawn lengthwise into three to five strips and the edges of these are then planed and glued together. After the glue is dry, the resulting board is then run through a planing machine which may take off as much as a quarter of an inch of stock thereby levelling the board.

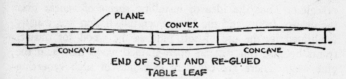

END OF SPLIT AND RE-GLUED
TABLE LEAF

FIG. 47. How a badly warped table leaf or table top can be sawed apart, re-glued, and put through a planer at a mill. Real old table tops and leaves are usually thick enough to take this treatment although this cannot be said of modern tables.

It will be clear that such an operation will destroy the natural grain pattern. Yet if one is bent on saving an old family piece with many sentiments attached to it, this may not be too important. It is also clear that this operation of reducing the thickness of a table leaf must be extended to the top of the table and to the opposite leaf, even though they are not warped. Otherwise the difference in thickness would be painfully obvious.

Fortunately most of the old cherry and walnut drop-leaf tables had very thick tops and the reduction of this thickness by a quarter of an inch or so is not a serious matter. So much for warping.

Oftentimes the amateur workman is called upon to repair veneer both on old and new articles of furniture. In the old days, especially during the early and mid-Victorian periods, crotch veneer, mahogany and walnut, was widely used especially on chest drawer fronts, console table tops and secretaires. The object was solely that of beautification and not economy, as one might think. The old cabinetmakers were

E

far too smart to attempt the construction of drawer fronts or table tops from solid crotch walnut or mahogany. Crotch wood is not strong enough for that but at these points in a tree the grain runs wild. However, when such wood is sliced thin as in the case of veneer, a beautiful grain pattern is revealed. Thus the idea of installing sheets of veneer over the drawer fronts and the like. Such installation was usually facilitated by the use of soft pine as the wood for drawer fronts because this was an open-grained wood that held the glue well. There are excellent examples of such veneering that has been on well over one hundred years and they show no signs of giving up the struggle to remain beautiful.

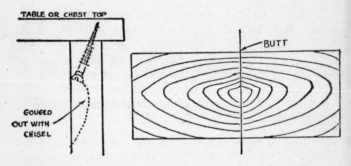

FIGS. 48 and 49. At left is illustrated the method used by old cabinetmakers to hold tops on chests of drawers and tables. The method is still used, save that the gouged recess is bored out. Sketch at right shows how beautiful patterns for drawer fronts or table tops are made by butting two matched pieces of crotch veneer.

The expensive, well-done chests had drawer fronts with matched end-to-end veneering as shown in Fig. 49.

This was·done by mounting two subsequent slices of veneer in such a way that a definite pattern would develop. Veneer sheets may still be purchased in this manner so that end-to-end mounting is possible.

Most modern veneering is done for the purpose of making cheap wood look expensive by placing over it straight-grained walnut or mahogany. The price asked for solid walnut or mahogany these days is beyond the budget of most families.

These modern veneers are usually put in place with plastic adhesives and here it might be well to warn the craftsman that the use of the powerful solvents used in paint and varnish removers might well lift such veneering by getting at the adhesive underneath. Old-fashioned glue is not soluble in these varnish removers.

The matter of repairing old veneering will be treated first. More often than not such repairs on table tops, drawer fronts and the like simply involve blisters (where for some reason or other the glue underneath a certain spot has failed to hold), digs and chips off edges. In any event, a careful job is called for if the repair is not to be too noticeable.

A blister has to be treated somewhat in the manner of a boil on a person—lanced with a very sharp knife, using an X cut. Little will be gained by simply running some glue or other adhesive beneath the resulting flaps of veneer and then pressing them down until the adhesive sets. No matter what adhesive is used, it will be necessary to first remove the old glue, both from the wood that held the veneer and from the veneer itself. This can be done with a special tool made by heating a ten-penny nail and flattening one end with a hammer on the anvil. This is then sharpened with a file and used to scrape out the old glue. One must be careful not to bend the flaps of veneer too much. Old veneer is brittle and may break very easily.

After the new glue or other adhesive is put in place

beneath the flaps, a piece of waxed paper is put over the repair and this is then covered with a perfectly flat block of hardwood. The clamp is applied to this. Incidentally this same clamping arrangement is also made for inlays described below.

Inlays are used to replace broken veneer on the edges of drawer fronts and table tops, also in the case of removing deep digs or heavy discolouration. The most important matter in making such repairs is the fit of the new piece. As for matching new veneer with old stuff either in colour or pattern, one will have to be satisfied with something far from perfect. Old veneer has a patina of its own, something that only the long years will bring. Therefore if the workman would better equip himself to make such repair on old veneered furniture, let him search for some hopelessly damaged piece of this type at country auctions. Oftentimes a hopelessly broken old chest with a veneered front may be bid in for 10s. or so and a ten-year supply of veneer for repairs bought with it. Usually the craftsman will wish only to take the drawers home with him if the rest of the piece is in bad shape. On the other hand, it is always to be remembered that it is nice to have on hand a supply of old wood of all kinds if one is in the habit of making repairs to old furniture.

Damaged spots in veneer must be first trimmed to some definite shape—square, oblong or diamond. Naturally one does not cut more of the edge away than is necessary to completely obliterate the damaged spot; the smaller the inlay needed the better, for one cannot hope to make a perfect match. Even if the colour is right, the grain stream will not coincide.

In doing this cutting, a very sharp knife, freshly sharpened, is used along with a steel straightedge as guide. Any wavy cutting by hand will make it impossible to cut a piece of inlay veneer that will not leave a big crack that will have to be filled with a preparation like plastic wood which will emphasise the repair by placing a different colour boundary around it.

The inlay is cut a trifle large and then the workman sets about cropping it down with his straightedge and sharp knife until it makes a perfect fit. It is then glued into position, using waxed paper, a block and a clamp.

Let it be assumed that the worker has before him a single drawer front of a Victorian bedside stand and that it has been treated with an original end-to-end veneer. He finds that one side of the veneer is damaged beyond recall. Will he replace the veneer only on one side? A good craftsman would be far more inclined to remove all of the veneer on the drawer front and replace it either with a single piece or an end-to-end mounting. If this problem presents itself in connection with an old chest with several drawers, only one of them in need of veneer replacement, the problem becomes a bit awkward. The best solution is to remove some veneer from an old chest front and place it on the single drawer.

It so happens that most old mahogany veneer is a deep red. If it is impossible to use old veneer in a case of complete removal, then one may use new veneer and there is a good chance of a colour match by using red mahogany oil stain, first in dilute form for it is better to have the new piece too light than too dark. The new veneer can very easily be made darker but it is not easy to make it lighter in colour.

A word about the removal of old veneer may be in order. The old varnish is completely removed first. Then the grain is opened by the use of No. 0 sandpaper. Rags soaked with water are then laid out on the piece and permitted to remain overnight. This will soften the glue underneath sufficiently to permit removal of the veneer when a sharp instrument like a chisel is used to gently pry it loose. If one wishes to save the old veneer, it will be necessary to work very carefully because old veneer is extremely brittle. After removal, the glue on the back of the old veneer is permitted to set up again after which the veneer is placed upside-down on a flat surface. A piece of No. 0 sandpaper on a block is used to sand off the old glue, making the veneer ready for re-glueing. To prevent undue curling and warping during the drying period, a piece of wax paper may be placed over the moist residue of old glue and the veneer held down by a flat board and weights.

When veneer is applied, no matter in what size, pressure

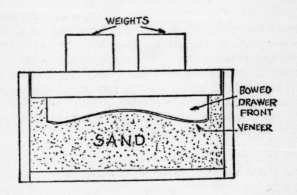

Fig. 50. How a sand box and weights are used to produce glueing pressure on irregular surfaces when veneers are being set in place.

glueing (or the use of any other sort of adhesive for that matter) is called for. For small pieces there is such a thing as a cast iron and steel veneering press. That is a luxury. A good substitute amounts to two flat hardwood boards and a set of clamps, two of them with throats large enough so that pressure may be applied to the centre of the boards as well as to the edges. Otherwise the centre portion of the veneer is not apt to be secured sufficiently well. To prevent the glue oozing from the edges and fixing itself to the clamping boards, a large piece of waxed paper is advised. Otherwise a joint might be effected and part of the veneer ripped off on the edges when the piece is released.

Attachment to a curved surface may be effected with a sandbox as shown in Fig. 50. The lid is given a fairly snug fit to prevent the sand from oozing out when pressure is applied, in this case usually with weights.

A continuous radius is treated with a set of cauls as illustrated in Fig. 51. Some careful fitting is needed in cases of this sort.

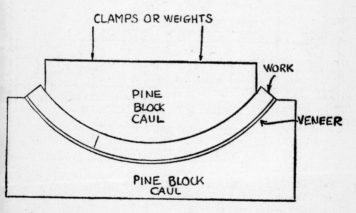

FIG. 51. How what is known as a caul is used in glueing veneer to curved surfaces.

As previously stated, modern veneers are often used in straight grain to give an appearance of expensive wood to ordinary wood. In the case of repairs to such veneered surfaces, matching is not as difficult as in the case of matching crotch veneers. All of these modern veneers may be obtained from the special supply houses advertising in the craft and mechanical magazines.

Oftentimes gouges and blemishes in veneered surfaces are too small to warrant an inlay. In such cases one of the plastic wood preparations may be used. Matching may be brought about by the use of oil stain or, in the case of plastic wood, with a colour varnish. This may be rubbed down later with pumice and oil to take the edge off the gloss.

SCREW NO.	2	3	4	5	6	7	8	9	10	12	14	16
L = LENGTH												
D – DIA. Max.		.103	.116	.129	.142	.155	.168	.181	.194	.220	.246	.272
Min.		.092	.105	.118	.131	.144	.157	.170	.183	.209	.235	.261
DRILL Hard Wood		.0550	.0650	0730	.0781	.0940	.0995	.1040	.1130	.1299	.1470	.1695
Soft Wood		.0410	.0492	0571	.0625	.0650	.0760	.0827	.0890	.1024	.1160	.1299

5/64 = .078125	5/32 = .15625	15/64 = .234375
3/32 = .09375	11/64 = .171875	1/4 = .25
7/64 = .109375	3/16 = .1875	17/64 = .265625
1/8 = .125	13/64 = .203125	9/32 = .28125
9/64 = .140625	7/32 = .21875	19/64 = .296875

Fig. 52. The various types of woodscrews, their numbers, drill sizes, etc.

No doubt the woodscrew chart (Fig. 52) will be of great assistance to beginners. Here are shown the various types of screw heads, screw numbers, lengths, diameters and the drill sizes to use for hard and soft wood. Decimal equivalents for the ordinary fractions are given below. This will help in the selection of twist drill sizes for the various screw diameters.

The matter of proper glueing is important for the amateur craftsman. Good glueing is easily possible nowadays with the specially prepared glues and other adhesives on the market. No longer is it necessary to heat animal glue with the consequent danger of either burning it and rendering it unfit for further use or applying it below the proper temperature only to have the joint upon which it is used come apart. Genuine hide glue, made by several reputable companies, is now available in liquid form and ready for immediate application without heating.

The reasons why any good glue or any one of the modern adhesives do not hold are easily outlined and the mistakes are easily avoided. Nowadays there is absolutely no excuse for poorly glued joints. On the other hand, neither is there any magic by means of which silly carelessness can be circumvented.

For one thing a joint must fit accurately and the contacting surfaces come together completely. That is one of the big secrets. Many joints are put together by amateurs where only a few points contact. Glue will hold properly only at these points. Hence such a joint will lack strength. The *whole* of the surfaces involved should come together. For instance, in the preparation of the edges of two boards that may form a leaf for a drop-leaf table, the worker persists until he can butt these edges together, hold the joint up to the light and see no light through it. Such a butt joint is not going to be had with a few strokes of a plane.

If such a joint is had, the rest is easy. One simply smears glue on the joint, the amount not being critical because the excess will be squeezed out when pressure is applied. In the case of prepared hide glue, one sees to it that the glue is not icy cold when the application is made. It should be on the warm side, certainly not below 70°. It is also assumed that the joint, no matter where, is perfectly clean and that the pores of the contacting pieces of wood have recently been opened by either sanding or planing. Grease, even in slight amounts, is fatal to glueing. Wood pores plugged with old glue or the residue of old wood finishes are also fatal.

The next thing of importance is plenty of pressure applied *evenly* during the setting-up period which lasts for twenty-four hours. Small joints may be placed in the bench vice.

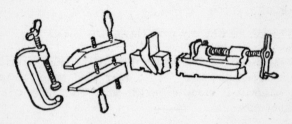

FIG. 53. The three types of wood clamps used in glueing. All come in various sizes. The one at left is wrought iron and is intended more for depth than width because of the shallow throat. The opposite is true of the wooden clamp at centre. Clamp at right may also be had in wrought iron. It will accommodate table tops, etc.

Larger ones may be set in the jaws of a series of clamps such as shown at the left in Fig. 53. Both types come in various sizes and the worker could use a set of four or more of each. Here the budget will have to dictate but there is this much to be said about this matter: Jerry-made devices rigged up to produce pressure may fail and several sets of clamps of various sizes amount to a good investment.

Where table tops and other work requiring glued edges of long boards are concerned, the type of clamp shown at the right of the drawing in Fig. 53 is used. The jaws of the type shown are adjustable along an oak beam provided with notches. Such an arrangement might be a trifle less expensive than the forged all-metal glueing clamps of the larger size. At any rate, at least a pair of clamps of either type should be in a shop. These clamps should have a capacity for work three feet across. Larger ones may also be had if desired.

If the worker wishes to use some of the modern plastic adhesives that have been prepared for home use, there is no reason why he should not. All of these materials are easily prepared and easily applied. Whether or not they will last as long as old-fashioned glue is a question Father Time will have to answer. Nobody yet knows.

DOES IT REALLY NEED REFINISHING?

The amateur restorer of furniture should not be too quick to condemn the finish on pieces that reach his hands for rehabilitation. There are certain remedies for scratches and digs, for stains, dullness, etc. And what, aside from a bit of time, has a man to lose if he attempts to restore an old finish and finds that, after all, the result does not please him? The answer to that question is found in a bottle of good varnish remover.

Whether or not a finish already present on a piece of furniture is worth trying to save will depend in a large measure upon personal judgment. Of course, if the digs and scratches are too deep and too numerous, restorative work would not be worth the trouble. Then there is the matter of very old varnish where the surface is covered with fine checks. This may be true of only a part that has perhaps been constantly exposed to sun coming in from a window. Unfortunately there is not a positive cure for such a condition. Some beginners may think that a heavy application of new varnish will fill these checks but this is not so. And the mere refinishing of a single checked side would produce a bad contrast with the rest of the piece.

In many cases, pieces of furniture come into the worker's hands after years in an attic or storeroom. They are covered with dirt and grease and gouges, but the finish still offers possibilities for careful workmen. The first thing to be done is to wash the piece thoroughly with warm water, a soft clean rag and soft soap, the gentlest of cleaning agents. It will help if three tablespoons of boiled linseed oil and one tablespoon of turpentine is added for every quart of warm water used. This is followed by wiping with a clean, dry cloth. Many a tyro has changed his mind after seeing the simple magic of a good washing. But this is not all that can be done to improve old finishes. Several applications of good furniture wax, with subsequent rubbing after each application, will help.

If, after washing, the worker finds that refinishing is not called for, he may further improve the surface by a gentle rubbing down using a very thin mixture of grade FFF pumice and crude oil. If crude oil cannot be had, then ordinary thin lubricating oil may be used. The cutting power of the mixture is reduced by using a small amount of pumice, say about a teaspoonful to three or four tablespoons of oil. Rubbing may be done with a piece of an old felt hat folded on itself several times. As will be noted from the instructions given for such rubbing later in this book, one must be careful not to cut through the varnish on the edges.

After the rubbing is completed, the surface may then be washed with benzene or untreated petrol and furniture polish or wax applied.

When there is a question as to whether or not an old finish can be brought back to a suitable condition, time will be saved if the workman will attempt the restoration on a small area—say a square 6 x 6 inches. If he finds this working out, then he may proceed to wash the whole piece and treat it with wax or pumice and wax.

In cases where old varnish is affected with tiny checks, the foregoing treatment may be modified a bit in a further effort to avoid the trouble of total refinishing. After the washing with soapy water, which must be done first in any case, the workman goes over a square of the finish with very fine steel wool, rubbing gently. This removes the top layer of flaky, dry varnish and much of the checked effect may be overcome thereafter by several applications of wax with hard rubbing. If the effect is satisfactory, then the treatment may be continued. If not, no harm has been done.

Those who feel that varnish may be placed over checked surfaces, are lacking in experience. No amount of varnish will overcome the defects of such a surface. And that holds true for either clear or brown varnish. In short, where total refinishing is indicated because of heavy checking or flaking, there is no magic short cut. If washing, steel wool and waxing a surface will not achieve the result sought then there may be only one alternative: total removal of the old finish in the most approved manner.

However, if the worker wishes to take a desperate chance in attempting to restore a badly checked varnish, he may proceed as follows, safe at least in the knowledge that if the treatment does not work, nothing has been lost but labour. The materials involved are not expensive and the work expended will not make the total removal of all of the finish more difficult if this is to be the final resort.

The finish is first washed with the warm water-soap-oil mixture suggested in the early part of this chapter. After the surface has thoroughly dried, it is treated with the following mixture, the worker first trying a small area:

Two tablespoons of boiled linseed oil are mixed with one tablespoon of turpentine. To this is added about one and one-half tablespoons of a good clear varnish. If the whole surface is to be covered, then a corresponding amount of the mixture must be put together using the proportions mentioned above.

The mixture is warmed in a bottle placed in hot water before it is applied. It is applied to a small amount of surface (6 x 6 inches) at a time and it is rubbed hard with the palm and heel of the hand. Rubbing continues until the surface becomes sticky and the hand drags. A clean cloth should then be used to remove the excess oil. After this dries, the process is repeated until a satisfactory condition may be had. This, however, may or may not come about, depending upon the condition of the original finish before the treatment was started.

Even the presence of deep scratches and gouges on old finishes does not necessarily preclude the possibility of bringing about acceptable restoration. The scratches may be skilfully treated to bring about almost total obliteration and gouges may be filled with stick shellac or other satisfactory compounds.

In the case of surfaces having many deep scratches, so many that individual treatment would be most tedious, then perhaps the worker should investigate the possibility of using what is known as an " amalgamator." This is a special preparation that may be had at any well-supplied paint store. Really, it amounts to a mixture of special solvents that is painted on the surface to be treated—a table top, for instance —and allowed to remain there. The varnish softens and flows and then re-sets. After it is hard again, the worker may rub and re-wax the surface. Best results are had with amalgamators when the varnished surface is hand rubbed with crude oil and pumice after the varnish has re-set firmly. Probably two or three days are necessary for this.

The trouble with amalgamators is that the varnish is very apt to set up extremely glossy. This condition, however, has a simple cure. The worker takes a piece of fine steel wool and goes over the whole surface, using just enough pressure to cut the gloss from the finish. Then this is followed by the application of good furniture wax and rubbing.

There are many methods of treating scratches, some of them good, some of them worthless. What the worker wants is a method that will make either a superficial scratch or a deep one as inconspicuous as possible. Oftentimes minor scratches may be treated by the simple (and old-fashioned) trick of rubbing them over with a nut-meat; walnut, for instance. However, this amounts to an ordinary household remedy and is not professional.

If the home worker has a variety of oil stains at hand, he can find one or a mixture of two that will produce the proper shade. Such stain may be purchased in small ($\frac{1}{2}$ or $\frac{1}{4}$ pint) cans and it is excellent for this purpose. The stain comes in maple, cherry, red mahogany, brown mahogany, walnut and oak. Many in-between shades may be had by proper mixtures of these stains.

The stain is used to cover the scratches, being applied with a tiny, soft brush such as children use for water colours. Excess is carefully wiped away from the edges of the scratch with a clean rag. After drying for twenty-four hours (oil stains are slow driers) the scratch is then covered with clear varnish (that is, if the piece of furniture itself is varnished) and this in turn is permitted to dry. When the varnish dries, a small piece of felt and a thin paste made up of crude oil and pumice is used to carefully rub the treated spot. This will cut the varnish down to match the surrounding old varnish. If thereafter the whole piece of furniture is varnished, it should be most difficult to find the scratch or scratches if a good colour match has been made. It should be remembered that oil stains dry out a few shades darker.

Some of the larger paint and varnish dealers or hardware stores carry various forms of scratch removers, many of them used with partial solvents and perhaps a small amount of very mild abrasive. All of these preparations that the writer has used have been found perfectly satisfactory.

Deep dents and gouges may be treated with what is known as stick shellac. Stick shellac is nothing but shellac mixed with colours and other materials and sold in solid stick form rather than in the dissolved form. The colours range from light buff down through several shades of brown and into red mahogany. A set of ten sticks of different shades will be found to be sufficient for all ordinary work. Such sticks may be had in short lengths at any paint supply house.

The procedure in applying stick shellac to dents and gouges follows: Naturally the worker first selects what he thinks to be the proper shade. He then melts this with a soldering iron, holding the stick to the iron directly over the dent and permitting the drops of molten shellac to fall upon the spot to be treated. The soldering iron must be just hot enough to melt the stick. Excessive heat will burn the shellac and destroy it.

Immediately the worker fills the dent to slightly overflowing with the melted shellac, he must smooth it out and level it. This is done with a small spatula gently heated in an alcohol flame. A candle flame will deposit soot on the spatula and discolour the shellac. The spatula should be hot and immediately ready for use.

After the shellac has been smoothed and has set (allow several hours) it should be rubbed gently with a mixture of petrol (be careful of lead-treated petrol; it is poisonous) and rottenstone. A piece of an old felt hat glued to a small block of wood is excellent for this purpose. While rubbing, the worker occasionally wipes the surface clean with a rag to see if the rubbing has proceeded far enough. Otherwise he may continue to rub until he has cut through all of the varnish surrounding the treated dent or gouge.

Other preparations may be used for filling dents and gouges. Here, of course, the mind of the worker may run to the modern preparation called plastic wood, which is a combination of a plastic binder and wood flour. While this substance has many uses and is invaluable for filling holes in surfaces

F

to be enamelled or painted, its use on varnished surfaces is not recommended. When supplied in natural wood colour, this substance dries out hard and non-porous. Hence it will not take stains and it is therefore very difficult to match it to the varnished surface on which it is used.

Of course, ordinary putty will dry up and eventually fall out of any indentation in which it may be placed. Sometimes a thick paste of varnish and pumice may be used to fill a dent. This is worked down, when dry, with pumice and crude oil using fine sandpaper first.

In many cases the worker will wish to cover the treated spot with varnish and then rub the varnish. However, if a careful job has been done with the stick shellac and good colour selection is had, this may not be necessary.

Another way of matching colour is to mix ordinary oil colours, such as used in painting, in clear varnish until the correct colour is had. A few drops of japan drier will also help. Several applications of this are put in place, allowing each to dry in turn. Rubbing is done with felt, rottenstone and crude oil. The oil colours to have on hand for such purposes include Turkey red, rose madder, burnt sienna, raw sienna, burnt umber, Vandyke brown and raw umber.

These colours are used in matching in the following manner:

For walnut one uses burnt umber or Vandyke brown. At times, a bit of raw umber may be added.

Oak calls for raw umber (for mission) and burnt umber for brown oak. Burnt umber and a little raw sienna are also used. Golden oak calls for raw sienna and a little burnt umber, the worker adding one colour to the other until the match is had.

Maple calls for burnt sienna for the redder forms of the wood and raw sienna for the yellow forms. Blends of in-between shades are made by mixing burnt and raw sienna.

Mahogany makes use of Turkey red, rose madder or rose pink. Oftentimes a little burnt umber is added. Brown mahogany calls for brown umber with the addition of a very small amount of Turkey red. Real dark mahogany needs Turkey red with the proper amount of black added. The worker starts with a very small amount and simply adds more until the right colour is had.

The white spot on varnished surfaces has long been the bane both of the housekeeper and the amateur refinisher. Such spots are caused by standing water, alcohol or hot objects left too long. To effectively remove such spots make a medium-thick paste of powdered pumice and linseed oil.

The application may be made with a soft, clean rag and the rubbing is interrupted occasionally for inspection to see if the white spot has been removed. Perhaps the paste will have to be wiped away with a rag soaked in turpentine before inspection can be made.

Inasmuch as the chemical nature of these spots vary a great deal with different varnishes and also with the substances that cause the spots, best effects are not always had with the paste mentioned above. In that event, perhaps one of the following may be used: (1) Table salt and light machine or mineral oil. The finger is used to rub. This is first moistened in the oil and then dipped into a dish of salt. The rubbing is gentle. (2) Another inexpensive paste may be had by adding pumice to camphorated oil or oil of peppermint. Only gentle rubbing is necessary.

PAINT AND VARNISH REMOVAL

Offhand a beginner might decide that there is little skill required in the successful removal of old paint and varnish. That in a sense is true when the modern solvents are used. Yet experience in the matter can provide certain discoveries that will save time, materials and awkward situations.

For one thing, the thrifty fellow is very apt to make the mistake of assuming that he has no need for some of the modern solvent preparations used in the removal of paint and varnish. Why spend 10s. a gallon for this stuff when one may use a solution of hot caustic soda and a piece of broken glass?

The danger involved in the use of the hot caustic soda solution should be enough alone to dissuade an amateur. This is one of the most corrosive agents known to man, attacking the flesh with great vigour and with disastrous results. In applying the mixture, the brush may slap and flip a drop of the solution into the open eye. Damaged sight to that eye will undoubtedly result. If the amount of solution reaching the eye is great enough and is not promptly removed, blindness can result. The other prospect is open flesh wounds that are difficult to heal. Not only that but hot caustic soda solution is also capable of destroying wood fibre and discolouring open wood. It makes the wood fibre soft and spongy and the caustic soda solution is difficult to remove entirely. The sensible workman shuns it.

Then there are those practical fellows who point to the use of a strong solution of hot trisodium phosphate. This is not dangerous but it is slow and sloppy and as many as five applications are often required when dealing with old paint. This, too, is apt to soak down into the wood and cause warping after a job is considered finished.

The modern solvents contain some members of the alcohol family with dissolved wax. The purpose of the wax is to prevent the solvents being absorbed by the wood where they would destroy the last vestige of oil, leaving the wood dry and lifeless.

In cautioning the user of these solvents, the writer can draw from experience. It is to be remembered that such liquids have the consistency of water. Therefore when a brush is slapped back and forth on a surface, it is apt to throw off large drops of the stuff. Should one of these strike the eye, instant pain will result as the solvents go to work. Impaired sight will result unless the eye is flushed out with clean water immediately.

On one occasion the writer received a large drop in his eye which was followed by immediate pain. Fortunately he stood near a water tap and thus was able to flush the eye free of the stuff. Since that time, he wears a pair of cheap goggles when using varnish removers. One good scare was enough.

These solvents should not be permitted to contact the skin of the body either. When they do, they immediately dissolve the fat and leave the skin dry. Too much contact with the hands will produce cracking of the skin.

The stuff is also dangerously inflammable with a flash point probably as high as the best petrol. That leaves smoking out during its use. It also argues for its use in open rooms with good air circulation. If possible, one retires to the open air with the job or to the garage. The manufacturers also advise against too much inhalation of the fumes from these solvents.

They have pronounced toxic effect when breathed too freely.

It is hoped that these remarks will not frighten the possible user too much. With reasonable care, the stuff may be safely used. The precautions are simple enough and there is nothing better in the way of varnish or paint removers.

To point up the proper usage of these solvents, it might be well to outline a messy and ill-advised procedure. Therefore it is assumed that a would-be user has a chest in the yard and that he is in the act of smearing it with solvent. Incidentally, the chest is standing in hot sunlight. The worker smears the whole thing at once making copious use of the solvent. Result?

Well, for one thing, the heat from the sun will evaporate most of the solvent before it has a chance to penetrate the paint or the varnish as the case may be. The grass below the chest will receive the drippings and be killed. On the shady side of the chest, the solvent will pick up some of the varnish and this will run down into the drawers, leaving deep stains on the inside and outside of the unpainted wood. Perhaps none of the varnish or the paint will respond to the scraper even after two or three such applications. The beginner is going to wind up having nothing complimentary to say about the so-and-so paint removers. Actually, he has made all of the mistakes that could possibly be made.

In treating a chest, the proper procedure is as follows: To prevent the dissolved varnish from running into the drawer crevices and thence to the inside of the drawers to produce unsightly stains, the worker first removes all of the drawers and treats the drawer fronts separately, taking care that the stuff does not run down the sides or over the lips. The secret here is a number of thin applications of the material to prevent running.

Another thing noted in the sad case of the beginner was that he treated the whole chest at once and applied the solution to the horizontal and vertical surfaces alike. Wherever possible, the workman tries to apply varnish remover to horizontal surfaces where it may be flushed on and allowed to stand. Such flushing will speed up the operation. Of course, where walls are being treated, one will have to be satisfied with slower progress using a larger number of thinner coatings.

Another mistake made by the fictitious beginner was his treating the whole surface of the chest at once. One should work only two or three square feet at a time. Larger surfaces will partially dry out before one can reach them with a wiping rag.

No set rule can be given as to the number of applications of solvent that will be needed before the wiping cloth or scraper is brought into play. The variables may be numerous. There is to be considered the nature of the varnish or paint, its age on the surface, the number of coats present, etc. The older varnish is the more easily removed. Usually just the reverse is true of paint. Age brings to it a flint-like hardness that may require as many as ten applications of solvent for complete removal.

After the remover has been left on for the required amount of time (usually about five minutes) the worker attempts to scrape the top layer off with a straightedge or a painter's broad-bladed scraper, wiping the removed material off on an old newspaper. If little is removed on the first scraping, one should not be discouraged, especially in the case of old paint. At least two applications will be needed even in the case of old varnish which is easily removed.

The solvent removers are not so expensive that one has to be too careful of their use. For instance, if after several applications which remove most of the paint or varnish, it is found that a final wash with the stuff will help, one should not hesitate. This wash, followed by wiping with old rags, will leave a perfectly clean surface save for the final removal of a thin film of wax which usually is taken off with a rag soaked in turpentine or mineral spirits. The removal of this film is extremely important no matter what sort of finish is contemplated. Many are the careless beginners who did not do this and later found that the lacquer or varnish they used did not dry out but remained tacky for days on end and wound up with a cemented film of dust on its surface.

The complete removal of varnish or paint from deep carvings can be a problem. Here the worker will be aided greatly by the use of old toothbrushes. These are dipped into the remover repeatedly and the solution is worked down into the crevices with considerable pressure. Such an operation should not be attempted without goggles to protect the eyes because a considerable spray will come from the brush bristles.

A soft brass wire brush of the finer type is much better than a toothbrush and the excess varnish picked up by it may be dissolved off by leaving the brush in the solution for a few minutes. A finely pointed steel instrument may also be used to scrape the varnish from the bottom of deep crevices. This may be ground to shape from an old three-cornered file.

Where varnish is to be removed from chair or table legs, each leg is in turn placed in a large tin can and the varnish remover washed over it repeatedly, the excess being caught by the pan.

During the past few years what is known as paste varnish and paint removers have come to the market and not a few workers have been won over to the use of such materials. For one thing the paste removers are not nearly as dangerous as the liquid mixtures. They may be used for reasonably long jobs (say an hour or so) in closed quarters, they are not as dangerous to the flesh, they may be controlled better and there is not a great danger from fire by their use. From a practical viewpoint, perhaps their most desirable quality is that of remaining on a vertical surface until they have done their work. Such paste material has no tendency to run whereas it is extremely awkward to attempt to use liquid solvents on vertical surfaces. They usually have to be repeatedly bathed with the solution.

After all the varnish has been removed, coarse steel wool may be used in place of sandpaper. This is followed by fine steel wool. It is perfectly safe to brush the fine wool over the carvings in any direction without danger of leaving deep cross-grained scratches.

The writer once heard of a workman who took a deeply carved piece of furniture to a monument works and had the varnish removed by the aid of a fine, low pressure sandblast. That is one way of doing it.

In cases where colour varnish, coloured lacquer or enamel is to be used on a surface from which old paint or varnish has been removed, then the worker does not need to worry about the removal of stains or the variations in colour left after the varnish or paint has been removed. On the other hand, if a nice surface of cherry or walnut lies beneath and a natural finish is desired with clear varnish, then it will be necessary to further dress the surface after the use of varnish remover and remove all blemishes as far as possible.

Real skill will be necessary in repairing gouges. Where brown varnish or enamel is to be used as a finish, one does not need to worry much about gouges. They may be filled with plastic wood or other such preparation. Where clear varnish or lacquer is to be applied, however, the problem is not so simple.

Plastic wood or other material of this sort will have a different colour than the wood upon which it is to be used and this colour variation will show through. As a matter of fact, plastic wood when dry has no absorbing power whatso-ever and the colour variation will be far more noticeable after the finish has been applied, due to the fact that the wood will absorb the oil from the varnish whereas the preparation used to fill the gouge will not.

Staining this treated spot to match the natural wood before the varnish or lacquer is applied is not as easy as it sounds. The writer knows of no way in which it may be done without detection. Sometimes a fair match may be had by mixing a slight amount of one of the dye stains with the plastic wood before the latter is applied. It is impossible to mix ordinary varnish with such material, however, for the simple reason that the material used as a binder for the wood flour is not miscible with the materials in the varnish, although the same is not always true of lacquer. In any case matching is not apt to be good.

The best solution of the problem calls for a tiny inlay of the same wood, using glue. To do this, it may be necessary to first remove wood in the vicinity of the gouge, making it deeper and wider. This is done with a small sharp chisel. Then a small piece of the same wood is cut from a place in the furniture where the depression left will not be seen. In the case of a table, this sliver could be taken from beneath the top. The sliver is carefully cut to size and made to fit in the enlarged gouge. In making such a repair, the worker sees to it that the top of the sliver rises above the surface of the board upon which it is used. Then, after the piece has been set in place and glued by the aid of pressure, a sanding block may be used to cut it down flush with the surface of the board upon which the repair has been made. A cleverly done job will then pass unnoticed. Such jobs are fussy and require skill and patience but they are the best answer to the problem.

In the case of naturally coloured wood like the various mahoganies, walnut, rosewood, etc., upon which clear finishes may be used, one should always bear in mind the use of stick shellac, which was described in Chapter 3.

If a refinishing job is to be done with clear lacquer, varnish or shellac and the absolutely complete removal of old finish is called for, it will be advisable to go over the surface of the furniture with medium fine sandpaper immediately after the use of the varnish remover. As has been said, no matter how carefully one works in the removal of varnish, a thin wax film is always left, being the residue that sets up and dries after the varnish remover has been used. What the worker will wish to do is to remove this final film. This is easily done at this time.

If stains are present, this will also be the time during which they should be removed. Some respond nicely and quickly. Others can be removed only with great difficulty and others not at all or only partially. Although not strictly in the category of stains, there is the matter of burns from hot flat-irons, cigarettes, curling irons and the like. If such burns are more than superficial and have a deeply charred surface, it is advised that such pieces be left alone. Really there is practically no remedy for a large deep burn. Even after the charred surface is removed, a deep brown colour will be left and the strongest bleaches will have only a mild effect. If a bleaching solution is too powerful, damage to the wood fibre will result and this can be disastrous, rendering a great deal of hard work useless. There is no perfect remover of stains; no miracle fluids are known. At best this can be nothing but a makeshift procedure.

In any case, one should first try to remove a stain with medium coarse sandpaper. Where hard, close-grained woods are involved, the chances are that the stain will not have penetrated to a great depth.

If such action succeeds only partially and there still remains a slight discolouration, then perhaps the use of a bleach will complete the removal. If it does not, the careful use of a scraper is called for. Naturally, there is a limit to the use of this instrument if a noticeable depression in the surface of the wood is to be avoided.

Oil and grease stains which are frequently met with may often be reduced or completely obliterated by alternate applications first of untreated petrol and then of bleaching solution. In the case of soft wood like pine, however, the penetration of the oil or grease may be so deep as to be beyond the reach of this procedure.

Where stains are exceptionally deep and are found to be beyond all of the remedies suggested in this chapter, there remains a last resort that is always effective if the board carrying the stain can be removed from the article of furniture. A table or chest top, for example, can always be removed and taken to a local timber yard where it can be slipped under a planer or a power sander. Oftentimes the removal of so little as $\frac{1}{32}$ of an inch of stock will expose a fresh clean surface and the colour left will be uniform. Let it not be forgotten however, that in the case of a drop-leaf table, both the top and the leaves must be put through the planer whether they need it or not. Otherwise two of the pieces will be thicker than the one that has been planed and they will also have a darker colour which would show with a clear finish. It might be said that any timber yard will render this sort of service for a shilling or two. There is nothing to beat it. If such a yard is handy and a worker is faced with stain removal even of a superficial nature, it is best to have it done in this manner.

However, the fellow in the small town will have to resort to other methods herein outlined. If a surface is found to be pretty well covered with a number of small, superficial stains, the following method of treatment will be found useful.

The bleach used is inexpensive and home-made although other preparations already mixed may be had at paint supply houses. To one gallon of hot water one adds ¾ of a pound of oxalic acid crystals which may be had at the local chemist. This will be enough to make a super-saturated solution. If all is not used, the solution may be bottled and used in the future. Some of the oxalic acid will crystallise out again when the solution cools but it will redissolve upon reheating.

The hot solution is brushed on the surface with a clean brush and permitted to remain there for four or five hours, the workman replenishing it as it dries away. At the end of the treatment period the remaining solution is wiped away with a clean rag and then the surface is carefully washed with linseed oil soap and clean water. A final rinsing with clean hot water is made.

The worker should not make the mistake of daubing the solution only over the stains. The bleaching action is fairly powerful and such treatment would leave a number of spots lighter than the main surface. Indeed in the case of stain being only on the middle top of a drop-leaf table that is to receive a clear varnish finish, both the middle top and the leaves should be bleached even though the latter are in no need of it. It is only in this way that colour match can be had if varnish is to be used later.

Tiny superficial scratches in soft woods may often be greatly helped by placing a soaked rag over them and holding a hot soldering iron against the rag until the water is partially evaporated. This steams the wood and causes a swelling of the fibres that does not entirely disappear.

The use of coated abrasive papers follows all varnish, stain and blemish removal. The choice of proper grits (grain size) is important. If a surface is still in bad shape even after treatment, then a fairly coarse grain paper is advisable. However, in no event should it be coarser than No. 0. The use of real coarse paper will leave deep scratches that will be difficult to remove.

Does it need to be said that one should avoid going across the grain of wood when using even the finest sandpaper? If the beginner should fail to respond to this advice, he will regret the trouble it will cause. Cross-grain scratches left by sandpaper are difficult to remove.

After sanding has been done with the No. 0 paper, the craftsman then turns to No. 00 which is finer and used for the final cut. In any event the paper is used over a small block of wood, say 3 x 6 inches in size. After the paper becomes dull, it may be brushed out with an ordinary scrubbing brush. Before the grains of abrasive material on any paper become dull, the paper is plugged with fine wood flour. Eventually the paper may also be turned 90° on the block which will expose the still-sharp edges of other abrasive material.

No home refinisher should be without steel wool in his shop, some fine and some coarse. When it comes to giving any wood surface its final treatment before the application of varnish, there is nothing to beat it. First the coarse wool is used and then the fine wool is applied. Both cut faster than might be expected and the wood is left with a lovely sheen. If one does not believe in the cutting and smoothing power of steel wool, let him do a small patch of wood in the above manner and then compare the patch with an untreated portion of the wood surface.

Both in the case of using sandpaper and steel wool, substantial quantities of fine wood flour will be driven down into the grain of the wood being worked upon. The best way to remove this is to moisten a clean rag with turpentine and wipe the surface with it. Dust, it should be recalled, is the amateur refinisher's greatest enemy.

THE VARIOUS SIMPLE FINISHES

There are many factors in finishing and refinishing. The market is so full of new products, both good and bad, that the beginner is very likely to get confused and subscribe to the use of materials or methods that are either inherently bad or beyond his skill. For a person without experience there are many dangers and effects desired are not always achieved.

Our discussion here will be divided into several parts; the refinishing of antiques, new wood and the refinishing of relatively modern furniture. The matter of antiques will be considered first.

Of course, before anything is refinished, the worker must make sure that the exposed surfaces with which he has to deal are scrupulously clean, as nearly free of stains as possible and that all wood dust has been removed from the pores of the wood. Where the use of most any sort of varnish is concerned, the beginner will find that his principal enemy is dust, airborne or from other sources such as dirty brushes, etc. Hence wherever possible amateur refinishers should seek varnishes that set up " dust-free " very quickly. This usually means that they pass the tacky stage within an hour or two. Naturally the longer the time required by a varnish to reach this stage, the greater the accumulation of dust. Thus the beginner cannot anticipate the depth of his troubles when he uses a slow-drying varnish and sets his piece up in the cellar beneath the living room where the constant passage of the occupants of the house cause a rain of dust particles. After the varnish has dried, he will find more than dust in its surface. Small pieces of matter will be deeply embedded and if they are removed they will leave tiny pockmarks. The effect will not pass muster with a careful worker and the whole surface would have to be treated over again.

In such cases it is not really necessary to strip off the new finish with varnish remover. The surface can be reworked with No. 00 sandpaper and then given a rubbing with steel wool. This done, the resulting varnish dust is carefully wiped away with a cloth moistened in turpentine. The worker then re-varnishes, taking advantage of his previous errors in judgment. If no other place than the cellar is available for the job, then he at least picks out a space underneath a little used room where a minimum of dust particles will be jarred loose from the floor. He might also wish to mop the floor of the cellar and to wipe the dust off surrounding articles with a damp cloth. Building a newspaper canopy on a slender frame to place over the freshly varnished article is also a simple and effective remedy.

True, many of the excellent, fast-setting varnishes supplied to-day do set up dustproof within a short time, but there is always a period after they are first applied when they are not dustproof. No matter what kind of varnish is used, precautions against dust should be taken. It is the perennial enemy both of the amateur and the professional refinisher.

Another thing: even dustproof or fast-setting varnishes can be delayed in setting up by certain atmospheric conditions like a super-saturated air. A freshly varnished piece of furniture tucked away in a wet cellar on a very humid day might bring a great disappointment. Such conditions are to be avoided. A warm, dry atmosphere will give any type of finish the best chance of setting up in minimum time and that is what every good refinisher seeks.

Oftentimes the clothes one wears are important, although that may sound perfectly silly until a case in point is mentioned. A friend of the writer's once attempted to refinish a certain antique treasure with varnish only to find that the whole thing had to be done over again because of dust. It wasn't surprising that this happened, for the man applied his varnish just after a long session with his power-driven sanding disc. Even though the disc was not in the building in which the refinishing was being done, the man's clothes were covered with fine dust and every movement he made shook some of it from his shirt and trousers. He just did not stop to think. The shirtless refinisher is apt to work best. It is said that many of the really fussy old coach painters stripped naked before they went in for the last coat. So much for dust.

Coming back to the piece of antique furniture, there are a number of choices of finishes both in colour and in texture. To help point matters up more, it will be assumed that the article is a Victorian ladies' chair in either walnut or mahogany. In the refinishing, walnut may be made to look like mahogany or the mahogany can be oil stained to look like walnut. Also the mahogany can be finished in any shade of the mahogany reds or the mahogany browns. Walnut can be made deep or light, etc. As to texture of finish, one may have the natural wood surface plus the oil stain and a little furniture wax, a semi-gloss or matt surface, a polished or a buffed surface that will shine like burnished copper!

Here it is to be mentioned that many amateur refinishers have no set notion of just the effect they (or, perhaps more importantly, their wives!) want before they roll up their sleeves and go to work on the basis of pure chance. The results are apt to be a bit disappointing.

Many mistakes of this sort may be avoided by a more thoughtful approach. If the chair is mahogany, why not first try a few experimental colour mixes on a scrap piece of

G

mahogany with friend wife in on the deal? All that is needed is a half-pint can of red mahogany and one of brown mahogany oil stain. A sample patch of full red, of full brown and several sample patches of mixtures of both may be made. These colours will change a bit when varnish or wax is placed over them but not much. In fact there is no reason why the varnish should not be applied over the sample colour patches. There is nothing sadder in this refinishing business than having a piece of furniture in the living room that " did not turn out just the way I (or ' we '!) expected."

If the plain stained surface is found to be satisfactory, then the finish is very simply accomplished. The oil stain is put in place and, after it has dried for at least twenty-four hours, the surface is gone over with a coating of a mixture of 50-50 turpentine and boiled linseed oil. This is sufficient to fill the grain of the wood and offer protection. It will take this several days to set but one does not need to worry about dust for this will not be a dust-holding surface. After the mixture has dried out, a light coating of good furniture wax will help. This can be rubbed up to a soft polish and with a pleasing effect.

In applying oil stain, it must be remembered that the depth of the colour will depend in a large measure upon the length of time the stain is permitted to remain on the surface of the wood before it is wiped off as per directions on the tin. Immediate wiping brings the minimum depth of shade. If the full and deepest colour of the oil stain is desired, then the stain is barely wiped off (just enough to give an even tone) and is left to dry. This may be a slow process requiring several days. In the latter case care is taken not to apply the stain in excess so that it will weep (run) and cause a streaky finish.

In any event where oil stain is used, one must make sure that it is perfectly dry and set before any varnish or other material is applied over it. Otherwise the varnish might pick up some of the stain and leave a blotchy surface. The oils used in these stains are miscible with the oils in varnishes. In the case of little stain being wiped off to obtain the right colour, forty-eight hours should be sufficient for drying. In case of not wiping off for full colour, several days may be required before it will be safe to apply varnish or even use furniture wax which will also pick up moist stain and carry it about, making the surface appear streaked.

The ordinary oil stains available at all paint stores and coming in shades of red and brown mahogany, yellow maple, red maple, light oak, dark oak and walnut, are by far the easiest to use, the easiest to blend for special shades and the easiest to remove if one changes one's mind before the varnish is applied. Dilution with turpentine is also easy. Such stains do not penetrate deeply and a hard wiping with absorbent dry cloth immediately after application will take most of an oil stain from a surface, especially from the harder woods. Fine sandpaper will complete the job without too much effort. Even after they have dried, such stains will quickly respond to sandpaper after the surface has been wiped with a rag soaked with turpentine.

Spirit stains, on the other hand, are extremely fluid and achieve deep penetration almost immediately after they are applied, making subsequent removal most difficult. It is also difficult to achieve an even tone with such mixtures. On the whole such stains are not well suited for amateur use and nothing more will be said of them in this treatise. Such stains, especially penetrating water stains, are apt to raise the grain of soft woods excessively, whereas oil stains have no grain-raising effects whatsoever.

It is possible for the home worker to mix his own oil stains if the simple ingredients are at hand. However, good oil stains placed on the market by houses of high repute are so cheap that there is little to recommend home preparation. For about

10s. one may lay in a good supply of all the common colours. It should also be remembered that such stains, being thin, have a large covering power. A half pint will go a long way. Another thing—if one runs out of stain on a job, a dried border line will not be noticed if the job is continued later.

In the case of the Victorian chair previously mentioned, clear (white) shellac or any good grade of oil varnish may also be used over the thoroughly dried oil stain but not, it must be remembered, without some darkening of colour tone. Those who are not experienced in this will find it difficult to estimate the nature of the tone after the varnish has been applied. It might be possible to finish a small patch of the flatter surface of the chair before proceeding with the complete finish. This can then be removed before the final finish. Oftentimes a spot underneath such a chair (the bottom edge of one of the stretchers for instance) can be sanded and re-finished as a test. It would not be necessary to remove this afterwards of course.

As to the choice between shellac and varnish over an oil stain, the favourable factors lie with the latter in everything but the easy application as it relates to dust. Shellac in any form does not provide a very durable finish. However, if it is used, it should be cut very thin* with shellac thinner, and at least five coats should be put on.

On the other hand, two coats of a good oil varnish would be quite sufficient. After each coat of varnish has been given the drying period recommended by the manufacturer on the tin label, fine steel wool should be applied gently to remove gloss. On the finishing coat, the pressure used on the steel wool should be a little heavier to bring about more cutting.

---

*What is known as "four-pound cut" shellac is sold mostly in this country. This means that four pounds of shellac are dissolved in one gallon of alcohol. This should be cut still farther in the workshop. A 50-50 mixture of this and commercial shellac thinner will be found suitable.

What is sought here is the reduction of gloss. The worker wishes to cut a matt surface. After this is done, the varnish dust left is wiped away with a water-dampened cloth and a good grade of furniture wax is applied and buffed. The same procedure is recommended in case shellac is used instead of varnish. The result is a rich semi-gloss finish, smooth and attractive, which may be repeatedly restored with a little wax. The finish should last a lifetime.

What recommends this sort of refinishing for antiques is its antique appearance. It avoids that "newish," over-finished look with the painful high polish.

However, in case a reader seeks this latter effect over an oil stain, it may be had with the following hard work: In such a case what is known in the trade as a rubbing varnish, which is tough and durable, is used. After the rubbing varnish has been permitted to set up for the time specified on the tin label, rubbing may begin.

This is done first with a mixture of pumice and crude oil, the mixture amounting to a semi-fluid paste. Mixing may be done in the top of a depressed paint tin, the worker mixing up more as he needs it. Otherwise the pumice powder will sink to the bottom and the mixture will not remain uniform.

Several thicknesses of an old felt hat may be used as the rubbing pad (thick rubbing pads are used for large flat surfaces and such felt may be purchased at paint stores by the ounce). The felt hat material will be pliable so that rounded portions can get down into grooves, etc. Some time may be required for the felt to soak up oil and pick up enough of the pumice and oil mixture. To facilitate this, the felt may first be soaked in pure crude oil and the excess squeezed out. This will make the felt still more pliable.

From this point the rubbing is begun after the felt is dipped in the mixture. One simply rubs with the grain, using moderate pressure. Too great pressure will cause the pumice to cut too fast. And here a word of caution that may save the whole job from ruin is in order. No matter what pressure is used, the pressure on the exposed edges of the furniture coming in contact with the felt will be far greater than that on the other surfaces. This is simple mechanics. Therefore the worker must *watch the edges* and rub them less, else he cut through the varnish and even the oil stain beneath it, leaving a light streak. That would be bad! He would be lucky indeed if he could re-cover such a spot with oil stain and varnish without leaving a tell-tale mark. At least he could try rather than refinish the whole job. Any corner, even on table top edges, must be watched hawk-like.

The rubbing procedure with the pumice mixture goes on until a soft, uniform gloss appears; a gloss less harsh than the original varnish. Good light is a necessity for such an operation.

This done, the excess rubbing mixture is removed from the surface with the aid of turpentine and then the rubbing is continued with a fresh felt pad and a mixture of rottenstone (much finer than pumice) and crude oil. This is continued until the gloss is increased to a suitable point. After this the surface is wiped clean with turpentine and the buffing continued with a pad of clean felt using considerable pressure. The operation is finished with a well-rubbed application or two of furniture wax. The result should satisfy the most insatiable craving for high gloss effects.

Some experienced workers prefer a mixture of water and pumice or rottenstone for rubbing. This is a dangerous mixture for beginners for the simple reason that it cuts too fast. True, it reduces the work required but its use is far more critical than that of oil and pumice. The oil tends to reduce the cutting action of pumice and therefore the beginner has more control left in his hands.

If at all possible only rubbing varnishes should be applied to surfaces that are to be so finished. Three days should be allowed for the setting up of this type of varnish which dries out very hard. Other varnishes can be rubbed but it must be remembered that they are cut very easily.

To achieve the very finest high gloss results by rubbing, each coat of varnish should be rubbed after it is applied and several coats should be put on. Not only that but, in the case of relatively open-grained woods such as mahogany and walnut, the basic foundation for the varnish must be improved by the application of wood fillers. To achieve perfection in such work, patience and hard labour are required. There will be more about wood fillers later.

Where a satin finish (in the writer's opinion the most beautiful and practical of all finishes) is to be had on such a thing as a table top, the worker may wish to substitute modern waterproof sandpapers in place of pumice. This sandpaper is exceptionally fine and it is used with clean water to reduce its cutting action. The action, however, is still very rapid and the worker is again cautioned about edges. Only a relatively few strokes are required by such paper, just enough to relieve varnish or clear lacquer of its gloss. Naturally one works parallel with the grain of wood to prevent cross-scratching. The paper is backed up with a small block of wood and a few tablespoons of water are first placed on the surface to be worked. The paper is worked from this water, the craftsman making sure that his paper is always carrying some water along with it.

It must be kept in mind at all times that this paper cuts very rapidly and that this is especially true with a non-rubbing varnish which is apt to be soft. There is no need of rubbing beyond the point where the desired effect is had. An occasional wiping off with a dry cloth will permit the craftsman to gauge this matter.

It invariably happens that a beginner will sooner or later wish to try his luck with some of the very modern plastic finishes or with some of the new lacquers especially if he is in search of a table surface that will not be affected by wear, alcohol, etc. No doubt these are excellent materials.

The plastic varnishes to be had are very easily applied even by amateurs. They set up dust-free within a relatively short time and they may be very easily rubbed to a satin finish with oil and pumice. Such finishes may cost a little more than ordinary clear varnish but not a great deal and they have much to recommend them. Applied to a surface, they give the exact appearance of any clear varnish.

Let no beginner think that he can apply either the plastic or lacquer varnishes over other varnishes containing organic materials. The powerful solvents in both of these finishing agents will immediately go to work on the varnish and within a very short time the article upon which they were used will be sad to behold. One may place varnish over the lacquers but never lacquer over the varnishes.

Once one masters the use of these fast-drying, clear lacquers, he has an ideal finishing material with the dust problem absolutely licked. Refinishing is greatly speeded up and a durable surface results.

It is speed of drying wherein the treachery of lacquer lies, at least for the amateur refinisher. With a slow-drying varnish, one may go back over the surface to touch it up a half-dozen times within an hour or so. Not so with lacquer! Within a few seconds it will begin to roll when brushed and then there is real trouble ahead, the only solution for which is a complete and messy removal of the entire surface.

For one thing, beginners are apt to use the relatively thick lacquer as it comes from the tin, whereas the secret lies in using a large number of very thin coats of lacquer cut with the thinner supplied by the *same* manufacturer. If one purchases one quart of lacquer, then he should also purchase at the same time two quarts of thinner. At least half and half should be used, and far more thinner than this in a spray outfit. As many as five or more coats of the thin mixture should be used on such a thing as a table top where there is a surface that must bear up under heavy use. However, the waiting period between coats is not long. Where several coats of ordinary varnish are applied with rubbing down after each coat, a whole week may be required to finish the work. On the other hand, five coats of clear lacquer may be applied in a single afternoon, so fast does this stuff set up ready for sanding with the new fine-grained water-proofed papers. Usually not more than twenty to thirty minutes is required between application and sand-papering. One simply makes sure that the surface is wiped clean and dry after each sanding.

Before the worker tries his luck with such materials, it is recommended that he practise a bit with thin mixtures and a brush of good quality. The brush, incidentally, should also be cleaned in the thinner, an extra quart being purchased for this purpose alone. Petrol is excellent as a brush cleaner for paint and a few other things, but it is strictly to be avoided with lacquer. It will cause this material to form a white, gummy substance on the brush. If one is to use lacquer, it will also be necessary, as in the case of shellac, to have one good brush set aside for this use only. If the brush is a little stiff from previous use, it may be softened within a minute or two by placing it in lacquer thinner.

Practice work may be done on a large board or other surface. Anyone can do a good job on a square foot or so. It is the big surfaces that bring trouble. With such surfaces, one end will set up before the other end is reached and retracing of steps to brush out a rough or uncovered spot will be fatal. Therefore if the beginner will take time out to give himself a few hours' training on trial surfaces he may easily catch the knack of using lacquer and then he will be in possession of an extremely valuable skill.

One does not brush lacquer out sparingly or with leisure. Lacquer awaits no miser or fussy worker. The brush is dipped deep, the immediate surface is flooded with the lacquer and the workman brushes furiously fast to achieve an even distribution before the escape of the solvents which are powerfully volatile. If the lacquer has been thinned sufficiently before the application, the procedure is not nearly so difficult as it sounds. In fact a certain state of mind might help. Let the worker not become panic-stricken before the application. It is for this reason that the application to a few experimental boards is recommended. The trouble is that ordinary varnishes dry by a combined process of oxidation and evaporation of oils. Lacquer has no oil and oxidation plays no part in drying. The old oriental lacquers, however, dried by evaporation and bore no relation to modern lacquers. The secret? Work fast!

The beginner should also see to it that he makes his first attempts with lacquer on perfectly horizontal surfaces to avoid weeping which, due to the high degree of fluidity, is easily possible with highly thinned lacquer. When finishing such things as tables or chests, it will be easy to keep turning the piece so that one side at a time may be covered, one always working on a horizontal surface.

While the use of waterproofed rubbing sandpaper is recommended for in-between-coats application of lacquers, perhaps the worker will obtain a little finer effect if he employs pumice and oil on the final coat.

While on the subject of lacquers, a word or two might be in order on the lacquers carrying colouring pigments. These are sometimes referred to as the lacquer-enamels and they are very fine materials indeed although all of the difficulties that apply to the use of clear lacquer also apply to them; hence they should be used in very dilute form. They may also be used safely on pieces intended for out-of-doors, like porch or garden furniture. Clear lacquer, on the other hand, will not stand up under outdoor conditions for reasons that will not be discussed here.

Black lacquer is especially fine to use on old Hitchcock type chairs which were originally painted black, green or grey to hide the fact that they were made of different kinds of wood. Little trouble will be had in handling lacquer on chairs because of the small amount of surface involved. If the final finish is a little too glossy, then a gentle application of fine steel wool followed by furniture wax is in order.

Oftentimes home workers come upon pleasing grains, as in the case of hard maple, which they wish to preserve as far as possible. The so-called " blonde " effects are also often desired (see Chapter 7).

Offhand one would guess that either clear lacquer or clear spar or other varnish would accomplish this blonde effect. This is not true. All of the finishes mentioned have a slight amber colour which is transmitted to the wood upon which they are used. This is deep enough to greatly darken the natural colour of the wood. What is really needed here is what is known as a water-white varnish to be found only in the larger paint supply houses. However, there is little reason why a local dealer, no matter how small, cannot order such a product. The worker seeking such finishes must bear in mind that even though he uses water-white varnish, gradual discolouration of the wood beneath, due to a slow photo-chemical action, will come about. The wood becomes darker with time.

As yet nothing has been said about the finishing of virgin woods—woods that have as yet been untouched by any finishing film. Of course if one finds a fine 18th century pine corner cupboard with a rich, nutbrown patina of natural wood, one ought to be arrested for even contemplating a refinishing job or the application of anything more destructive to the old surface than a clean dust cloth, or at most a washing with soft soap and warm water.

On the whole, new woods are different than woods that have been varnished or painted and from which the paint or varnish has been removed. Something happens to the latter; something that cannot be removed without the removal of surface wood to a considerable depth. This "something" relates to a stuffing or filling of the pores of the wood with varnish or paint as the case may be.

Pre-finishing treatment of new wood depends upon the nature of the wood and especially upon the nature of the grain whether open (coarse) or closed (fine and tight). It will usually be found that the harder woods, like maple and birch, have fine, hard surfaces while the softer woods like pine, chestnut and some of the mahoganies (it all depends upon where the latter are grown) have very open grains. Here it is to be pointed out that no ultimate surface, no matter how hard one works with rubbing, can be any better than the surface with which one starts. It would be nice indeed if someone would invent a varnish or other finish that would level off the microscopic irregularities of open woods but so far nothing of this sort has appeared. It therefore becomes necessary to use other means on coarse-grained woods but only in case fine buffed effects are sought.

If one made a reproduction of an old 18th century pine piece, then elaborate preparation for finish would be silly because the prototype did not have such a finish. (Antique finish on old and new pine will be discussed later.)

Some of the softer woods such as chestnut and the harder ones such as oak have deep grain. However, there is a simple and lasting beauty to oak with natural finish, although the same thing cannot be said of chestnut, a wood widely used in cheap furniture during the late Victorian period. Many tables, chests and beds, and some chairs, were made of it. If possible, the amateur will do well to avoid this wood.

Woods with open grain are often treated with a substance known as wood filler, which amounts to a paste used in different colours, different ingredients and different consistencies, depending upon the conditions to be met. When wood fillers set up, they should be hard but still able to take finishing material.

The coloured filler is also able to serve in two ways: it fills grain and substitutes for a stain. Indeed its function as a stain needs close study by those who seek a certain shade or tone for their work. Where colourless filler is employed, the worker may exercise complete control over ultimate colour by the choice of the correct oil stain, but where one of the standard ready-mix coloured fillers is used, little control may be exercised over ultimate tone and colour. Again the writer recommends to the beginner the advisability of using a few test pieces before he smears up a job with something that he will not like.

There are three principal types of wood fillers. One is transparent and is used on the better grades of wood where the cell opening or grain channels are so small as to be invisible to the eye. Use is indicated on such wood only when the worker seeks the finest finish requiring a high buff. For an ordinary satin finish, there is little need for such preparation. Really such so-called fillers amount to little more than a sizing. The experts, when seeking flawless results, use such filler material on even the better grades of mahogany, walnut, etc.

In the earlier days, filling such wood was often accomplished by repeated applications of a drying oil such as linseed. Each application was followed by a long period of waiting for oxidation and then rubbing. The application of linseed oil always darkens any wood and many applications darken it still more. This procedure of wood filling is no longer recommended.

If a reader of this book desires to take his chances in producing the ultimate in a highly buffed surface, he may bring about a good foundation for his labours by applying clear shellac, highly cut, as a wood filler on the woods with finer grain. At least a 50-50 mixture of the shellac thinner should be used with shellac as it comes from the tin. Two coats with very light sanding between using No. 000 paper are advised. About six to eight hours should be allowed between coats to avoid a gummy effect in the in-between sanding operations. It will be understood, of course, in the case of using oil stain, that the stain must be applied before the shellac.

The liquid fillers (the shellac is in the so-called transparent class) are not used a great deal in refinishing furniture except on woods like chestnut where grain is enormously large. These fillers are excellent for such use and also as fillers for new, open grain woodwork in homes. Such fillers are painted on in the manner of varnish and they do not have to be rubbed off as in the case of the paste fillers which will be treated next.

Paste fillers contain drying oils and a material like silex. A gallon of such stuff will cover about 250 square feet. It can be purchased ready mixed. It is recommended that all such fillers be followed by the use of No. 00 sandpaper after they have set up. If a wood such as pine is to be varnished, the use of this filler is indicated.

As before stated, most woods, and this goes even for some of the less desirable grades of mahogany, require the use of a paste filler. The solid material used in such fillers may be one of a number of things but the better wood fillers sold in tins usually have a form of silica called silex as the solid material. This is carried in a thick mass and may include such other materials as boiled linseed oil, japan drier, turpentine, naphtha, benzene, and colouring matter. As supplied by the trade such fillers are usually far too thick for use and must be thinned by the addition of turpentine or benzene.

These paste fillers are usually supplied in white or the following colours: ebony, red, brown, light and dark mahogany, natural or transparent, antique, golden oak, walnut and dark oak. Painters' pigments ground in oil are used as colouring material in paste fillers.

In a very large measure, the colours in which paste wood fillers are supplied indicates the woods upon which they are to be used; the brown mahogany on wood of that nature and colour, the red mahogany for red mahogany, etc. White filler is intended for general use where colour varnish or fine enamel jobs are to be used on open-grain woods.

Beginners are very apt to underestimate the degree of skill required in the successful application of paste wood fillers. For one thing, if any large amount of work is to be done with wood fillers, then it might be advisable to purchase a special brush intended for this use solely. A stiff, coarse brush is best so that the thinned paste will be pushed down into the cell and grain openings.

Before a paste filler is applied, the wood flour from all previous sanding must be removed from the grain where it is impacted. Otherwise plugged grain will greatly interfere with the successful use of the filler. An ordinary small scrubbing brush may be used to remove wood flour, the workman pressing down rather hard and always moving parallel with the grain. The final residue of dislodged wood flour is removed with a clean, slightly damp cloth.

There are many ways of using paste fillers, some of them involving surfaces that have already been coloured by water or oil stains. Such use requires a judgment and skill that must come with experience. The beginner is advised to confine his use of such fillers to the treatment of deeply grained surfaces where he either wishes to apply a smooth coat of enamel or colour varnish or to preserve as far as possible the natural colour of a coarse-grained wood such as mahogany or walnut by the use of a clear varnish. One should proceed very cautiously, however, where either the clear or coloured lacquers are to be employed over surfaces that have been treated with wood fillers. The powerful solvents in such materials may lift up some of the oils in the filler and give a muddy, unwanted effect. It is difficult in this treatment to provide an all-inclusive answer to such a problem. Any of the oil varnishes are safe to use but the expert at the paint store should be consulted in connection with lacquer because formulas of materials vary. Only a warning can be issued here.

In determining the degree of thinning that must be had before a paste filler is applied, the worker should be guided by the directions on the tin. Error in making the mixture too thin by the addition of too much turpentine is to be preferred over producing too thick a mixture that will not flow down into the wood grain. The slight damage coming from too thin a mixture may always be repaired by a second coat of the same consistency. It is an invariable rule that relatively thin mixtures should be placed on wood with small grain and thicker applications made on wood with coarse grain. In no case should the consistency be thinner than that of undiluted varnish. If the mixture drops too quickly from the brush, it is probably too thin. On the other hand, if it shows no inclination to drop from the brush at all, or very slowly, it is probably too thick.

In the application of wood filler of this type the workman seeks to overcome his habits of economy by failing to brush out the mixture. One always sees to it that paste fillers are put on in healthy excess. Also the mixture is constantly stirred to keep the solid material in suspension.

While some of the old-timers insist that paste fillers should be applied in the manner of varnishes, that is moving the brush with the grain, others insist that the paste should be brushed across the grain. With no claim to being an expert, the writer takes a more logical position. To ensure the filler reaching the very bottom of the grain, the first brushing should be with the grain. This is followed by a second brushing across the grain which should fill it.

The length of time a paste filler is allowed to set up before the excess is removed from the surface of the wood is important. Otherwise the removal of the excess may take out some of the impacted material and leave an indifferent surface. Here it is advisable to read carefully the directions on the tin.

In any event, the excess of paste filler is removed by brushing *across* the grain with a heavy piece of clean burlap. This subjects the wood filler to a cross-wise, shearing action which makes its surface flush with the main surface of the wood upon which it is used. It will be seen that even a small amount of lengthwise rubbing will be bound to dislodge some of the filler in the grain.

As a general rule, although the direction on tins in which wood fillers come may advise differently, one does not attempt to remove excess filler until the slight gloss has disappeared and the material no longer appears wet.

In the event of using such a filler on carved surfaces, extra care will have to be exercised in removal. In such cases it might be possible to work with a small piece of burlap or with a discarded toothbrush for the crevices.

All surfaces are somewhat rough after the filler has dried. It is therefore necessary to go over them lightly first with

H

No. 00 sandpaper and then with No. 000. This is used on a soft under-surface to prevent cutting through the film of filler. The little sanding tools in which abrasive cloth is placed over a base of sponge rubber are excellent for this purpose. A thick pad of cloth glued to a block of wood will also serve nicely and such a soft sanding block is convenient to have about the workshop.

As a final operation to such a surface, a cloth soaked in untreated petrol, benzene or naphtha is used to carry away the filler dust left by the sandpapering.

In the case of borderline woods with grain that is not especially coarse or fine, the use of a paste filler might be depended upon whether or not a water stain was used. Water stains raise the grain of wood a great deal and therefore may place a piece of wood in need of filling.

The following table may help a beginner to decide whether or not he will need to use a filler and what type it should be for the finishing job at hand:

Use Shellac or Other Liquid Filler	*Paste Filler only with Water Stain— Otherwise Shellac or Liquid Filler*	*Paste Filler of Proper Colour*
Basswood	Beech	Ash
Cedar	Birch	Beech
Cypress	Boxwood	Elm
Ebony	Cherry	Chestnut
Fir	Cottonwood	Mahogany
Hemlock	Gumwood	Locust
Holly	Maple, hard and soft	Oak
Magnolia	Sycamore	Rosewood
Spruce	Redwood	Walnut (all kinds)
Pine, both yellow and white		Hickory
Poplar or whitewood		Satinwood
Deal		

As a mixing guide for thinning wood fillers the worker may use the following table supplied by one of the manufacturers of such materials:

LIGHT MIX		MEDIUM MIX		HEAVY MIX	
Paste	Thinner	Paste	Thinner	Paste	Thinner
5 lbs.	2½ pts.	5 lbs.	3 pts. 5 oz.	5 lbs.	5 pts.
1 qt.	1 qt.	1 qt.	2 pts. 10 oz.	1 qt.	2 qt.
1 pt.	1 pt.	1 pt.	1 pt. 5 oz.	1 pt.	2 pt.
1 lb.	½ pt.	1 lb.	10½ oz.	1 lb.	1 pt.
½ lb.	4 oz.	½ lb.	5¼ oz.	½ lb.	½ pt.

If stirring is not constantly resorted to, the filler applied to the last of a large surface may be much thicker or thinner than that applied first, depending upon how deeply the workman had gone into the bottom of the tin.

The filler in any event should be brushed out, using a rather stiff, stubby brush. The material is applied with the grain and the worker should not cover too great a patch at one time. It would seem that about eight square feet would be sufficient. Otherwise, especially where naphtha has been used as a mix, the filler first applied is very apt to reach a stage of dryness where the proper removal of the excess will be most difficult. One seeks a uniform surface here just as in the case of using a varnish or enamel.

It will be noticed that immediately after the filler has been applied it has a slight gloss to it. As this is replaced by a dullness, the filler is ready to remove. It is usually recommended that fillers be left in place no longer than a few minutes. Thus the worker may find himself towing off (wiping off) at one end of the job (the first) while the last filler applied to the piece is not yet ready. One watches for the dullness to appear and goes to work immediately.

This so-called towing-off is done with a piece of burlap, tow or any other suitable material of this nature. Inasmuch as a thin film of filler left after the towing or wiping will soon set up hard, the worker should not plan on returning to a spot. Rather he should finish his work as he moves along, at all times wiping across the grain to produce a shearing action which will leave the filler deposited in the grain. Frequent changes of wiping material may be necessary for larger surfaces.

If the worker should be caught off guard and finds himself up against a patch of filler that has set up too hard, then he should moisten this with an application of naphtha followed by a second application of filler. This is then removed in the approved manner after becoming dull in appearance.

In the case of corners or lightly carved surfaces, a pointed match stick should be used to remove all excess material before it has had a chance to set up.

After the towing-off process, a final wiping is done with a soft rag. This should follow the towing off immediately and before the residue of filler has had a chance to set up. It might help to moisten the soft rag with naphtha as a final wipe. All of this wiping may be done with and across the grain for this really amounts to a cleaning-up operation.

A quick-drying filler in which naphtha has been used as a thinning agent should set up in about eight hours. A slow-drying filler, using gum turpentine, may require as many as thirty-six hours for setting up.

After setting up, the filler is sealed with a very thin coat of shellac or lacquer sealer. It is to be pointed out here that many fillers made during the past four years are available both for over-coats of lacquer or enamel. After this sealer coat has dried, it is sanded lightly with No. 000 sandpaper. After the dust has been brushed away, an undiluted coat of the final finish, whether lacquer or varnish, should be applied. This is a foundation coat and should therefore be rubbed with waterproof sandpaper of a very fine grade. Then the final coat of varnish or lacquer, as the case may be, is applied.

As before stated, ready-mixed wood fillers may now be

purchased in all the common colours as well as natural and white. It is quite possible that every worker will be able to purchase just the right colour for the job at hand. If he cannot do this, it is easy to change the colour of natural or white wood filler with the addition of suitable oils and pigments. It may be that a mahogany filler already at hand is to be made darker. In any event, procedure is as follows:

Ordinary oil colours are first mixed in turpentine, the worker bearing in mind that a small amount of such colour goes a long way and that it is better by far to err on the side of too little than too much. The thinned oil colours are added to the wood filler after it has been thinned and the worker stirs patiently until he obtains perfect uniformity.

Although considered a short-cut, some workers mix ordinary oil stains with wood fillers before the latter are applied. This may save the trouble of placing a coat of stain on the work before the wood filler is put on.

Here it is pointed out that it is often possible to produce attractive two-tone effects by using masking tape for stripes or borders before the wood filler is applied. Finishing goes forward up to the first coat of varnish before the tape is removed in time for the wood beneath to receive the finishing coat of varnish or lacquer.

In the case of raised grain, filler has not been given sufficient drying time. Pinholes may be caused by the filler being too thick and grey pores result from lack of sufficient drying time and from the filler being too light in colour. Of course, streaky or cloudy effects are due to poor wiping.

No filler is needed for woods such as basswood, cedar, cypress, fir, hemlock, pine, poplar, spruce or willow. A thin filler is usually advisable for alder, beech, birch, boxwood, cherry, ironwood, maple or sycamore. Medium fillers may be applied to butternut, mahogany (of certain grades), rosewood and walnut. Thick fillers are required by ash, chestnut, locust, oak, teak and the softer mahoganies with large grain.

In case the worker does not have data on the proper colour mixtures for colouring fillers with ground oils, the following will help:

BLACK: Add drop black to natural filler. Suitable for blackwood, or dark mahogany.

WHITE: Colour natural base with zinc oxide. Used for limed oak and similar effects on chestnut and ash.

LIGHT BROWN: Tint with Vandyke brown to required shade. Can be used on any light brown-colour wood.

DARK BROWN: Vandyke brown with a touch of drop black. For walnut, mahogany, etc. Suitable for any medium to dark-colour wood.

WALNUT: Half and half Vandyke brown and burnt umber.

LIGHT RED: Use any red colour (Indian red) in oil or japan, toning darker or lighter with drop black or zinc white.

DARK RED: Equal parts of burnt umber and rose pink. Add drop black for darker shade. Used for Sheraton mahogany or any other red finish where dark pores are desirable.

AMBER: Tint natural base with yellow or orange oil colours. Suitable for ambered walnut, harvest wheat mahogany and other bleached finishes.

To recapitulate, really only two types of finishes have been discussed up to the present. Both are placed either over oil stain of a colour to be chosen by the worker or over a plain mahogany or walnut chair (or other articles of the same woods, for that matter) without previous use of oil stain.

In the one case, varnish or shellac is placed over the oil stain and the surface left by either one of these is cut with fine steel wool and later waxed. In the second case where a buffed, high-gloss surface might be required, the use of an oil-pumice rub followed by a rottenstone-oil rub is recommended.

In either case, the inexperienced worker can proceed with a feeling of confidence in the outcome. He can be sure of substantially beautiful results, especially in the case of the first finish where the satin effect is brought about by the use of fine steel wool and furniture wax. Even a high-school boy could apply such a finish with ease. This is really an ABC finish. Either lacquer or the new bakelite-base varnishes may be employed in place of the shellac or varnishes if the worker desires.

A few words about brushes might be advisable at this point. If the best work is to be done just any old brush will not do. Here quality counts. One would rather own three or four really good brushes than two dozen from the sixpenny store. Then, too, there is the fact that a good brush may be rendered useless for further good work after its first job if it is not properly cleaned and put away.

First, what makes a good brush and how many types of brushes does a home shop need? As for size, the matter is simple enough. In the case of a varnish brush, size is determined solely by the work to be done. A man constantly varnishing large floors would not wish to use a small brush such as an amateur might employ for his cabinets or tables. In most cases the furniture refinisher will not wish to go beyond two inches in width.

In a large measure, good bristles make the good brush. The good brush does not bush out at its ends but has a slight taper. The bristles are firmly anchored through a well-designed ferrule and in rubber cement. Cheap brushes constantly lose their bristles by pulling as they move over a surface. This can be far more than awkward when lacquers are being used.

Perhaps the worker does not need more than three or four brushes to start with. Cheap brushes may, of course, be used to apply flat undercoatings, etc. If only clear varnish is to be used, then the worker should have a good two-inch varnish brush reserved solely for this use. If shellac is to be used, then a good brush should also be reserved for this purpose only. If the colour varnishes or enamels are to be used, then each should have reserved for its use a separate brush. The condition in which these brushes are kept will in a large measure determine the ultimate success or failure of the job at hand.

For one thing, no matter what material or brush is being used, the brush should be cleaned thoroughly in the proper solvent immediately after it has been used. First the excess paint or varnish should be removed by scraping the brush lengthwise and on both sides over the edge of the tin. Then a rag should be used to remove as much more of the excess as possible. Brushing out on a rough board will also help. What one seeks above all is to release the paint or varnish in the heel of the brush near the ferrule. If it dries there, it will later flake out when the brush is being used and particles will speck work being done.

After this preliminary cleaning, the brush is worked over with the proper solvent which will be mentioned soon. First comes a good flushing in plenty of clean solvent. Then the brush is combed out lengthwise with a fine wire brush, plenty of solvent being applied. One works especially up near the heel, where accumulations are most apt to form due to the fact that the bristles are most tightly pressed together at this point and paint or varnish is most difficult to remove here due to capillary effects.

After the combing, the brush is again rinsed thoroughly in solvent and wiped as dry as possible with a clean, lintless cloth. A piece of waxed paper is then placed around it covering all parts of the bristles, a rubber band or two is slipped in place and the brush is stored in a drawer.

This sounds like a bothersome procedure and it no doubt

is, but nothing less will do if the worker is going to produce good work without the necessity of buying a new 10s. brush for each job.

The solvents to be used for cleaning brushes follow:

Brushes used for paint, oil-base enamels or oil-base varnishes may be cleaned with benzene, white untreated petrol, naphtha, paraffin or turpentine.

Shellac brushes may be cleaned in denatured alcohol or one of the prepared shellac thinners now sold in the paint stores.

Lacquer brushes may be cleaned with the lacquer thinners. If this is not at hand, ordinary varnish remover may be used, with a final rinse in denatured alcohol. The worker is warned away from petrol for this purpose.

OTHER SIMPLE FINISHES

One method of refinishing was described in the preceding chapter. This involved the use of oil stain, varnish, the application of steel wool to relieve the varnish of its high gloss and the final application of furniture wax. Such a finish is easy to handle, it is durable and requires a minimum of time. A number of the writer's friends have tried it and it has yet to backfire if the worker has been careful about the dust problem.

There is another finish easily handled by amateurs that will give equally pleasing effects and it is without a dust problem. Reference is made to what is known as an oil finish. Boiled linseed oil, turpentine, a large quantity of clean, lintless rags and a lot of " elbow grease " and patience are the only things required to produce what many believe to be the most beautiful of all the finishes. This may be especially true for antiques.

One precaution is necessary. Even when diluted with turpentine, linseed oil, boiled or raw, will greatly darken the colour of any wood upon which it is used and over the years still more darkening will be had. Therefore the worker should give due consideration to this point and make certain allowances. For instance, he may wish to finish a piece of very light mahogany with the oil process outlined below. Not having had experience with such a finish, he may decide that the mahogany needs a bit of red or brown stain to darken its

118

shade before the linseed oil is applied. Such a darkening will doubtlessly turn out to be unnecessary and might make the wood so dark as to be unattractive. This business of anticipating the ultimate colour of any surface after a finish has been applied is tricky. Again it is suggested that any finish be applied first to a sanded spot inside the frame of the furniture upon which it is to be used. This will give the worker a preview of his ultimate colour and also the opportunity to change his mind.

Naturally all prefinishing operations should be done on the open wood before one sets out to apply oil finish. This may include the use of wood fillers, etc.

The mixture of boiled linseed oil and turpentine used in producing an oil finish is in the proportion of $\frac{2}{3}$ oil and $\frac{1}{3}$ turpentine. This may be used warm or cold, the warming permitting the oil to dry faster. Penetration is also deeper with warm oil. If heating is decided upon, it should be done in an old double boiler to reduce the danger of fire.

The oil and turpentine mixture is applied generously to the open wood and rubbed in with clean rags for about twenty minutes. Then the excess oil is wiped away with clean cloths. If carving or other deep crevices are present, care must be used to remove excess oil here also. Otherwise the oil will oxidise (gum) and later removal will be difficult.

With the oil finish it is advisable to work with only one surface at a time. For instance, on a chest the worker makes the first application of oil and turpentine to the top. Then, after this is rubbed for the first time, he turns the chest on its side and makes another application, working around until the whole surface is covered. After this has set up properly he starts all over again because the oil finish requires a number of hand rubbings and oil applications.

The simple secret of a good oil finish is plenty of rubbing of the sort that develops friction and heat. This means rubbing to produce pressure. The material used for rubbing is also important. As a case in point, pieces of clean linen grain bags are excellent for this use. Heavy woollens are also good. Either the heel of the hand may be used to bear down on the rubbing pad (the cloth, whatever it is, is folded over on itself several times) or the cloth may be wrapped around a stiff scrubbing brush. It is well to note in connection with this oil finish that one cannot overrub. No harm will be done if one rubs for one hour in place of thirty minutes. Indeed a better sheen will be had with the longer rubbing.

The ultimate beauty produced by an oil finish depends upon the degree of rubbing between coats or applications of oil and the number of coats or applications, the more the better, within reason. Certainly one would not wish to stop at less than five applications of oil, each with rubbing periods of from thirty minutes to one hour.

One of the main factors in such finishing work is the length of the set-up period between the applications of oil. This will depend in a very large measure upon weather and atmospheric conditions during the set-up period. If the article being finished is in a warm, dry room, two days should be allowed before the second coat of oil is put on and rubbed in the manner described. On all succeeding coats, however, at least a full week should be allowed in a warm, dry room before another coat is applied. If it is necessary to leave the article in a cold, moist room, then at least a month should be allowed between applications. It is clear that the rubbing should be as even as possible so that one part will not have a greater sheen than another.

If, before any application of oil is made after the first one, it is found that any oiliness or stickiness remains on the surface, then the next application of oil can be delayed until this stickiness completely disappears. The last application and rubbing is followed by an application of furniture wax.

One of the advantages of the oil finish is the ease with which it may be quickly restored to its full bloom by merely applying a single coating of oil and giving it a good rubbing with the same technique as that used when the original finish was produced.

This description of the oil finish may sound very simple, but the directions given above are complete. Anyone of the oil stains may be placed underneath such a finish if desired.

There is still another old-fashioned finish that may appeal to the beginner. It is just a bit harder to handle than the oil finish described above but it has the advantage of being applied faster. Here the ingredients are varnish, linseed oil and turpentine.

The mixture is made up with the following proportions: $\frac{1}{3}$ good waterproof varnish such as used on interior work, $\frac{1}{3}$ boiled linseed oil and $\frac{1}{3}$ turpentine. Another mixture such as that which is used for the plain oil rubbed finish just described is also put up. This is used first and two coats are applied in the same manner as for plain oil finish with plenty of rubbing.

When the second coat of the plain oil finish has been applied and permitted to dry after the usual rubbing, the oil-varnish-turpentine mixture is flowed on, the worker not stinting in its application. A continuous rubbing is maintained until the surface becomes tacky and the mixture begins to set. This may happen within twenty minutes or it may take an hour, the rubbing going on in the meantime. Naturally one will have to change arms occasionally or rest for a few minutes in case the tacky state is not reached before an hour has passed. All excess finishing material is wiped off at the end with clean rags and then the tacky surface is given ample time to set up and dry. This operation, as in the case of the plain oil finish, is repeated until a beautiful satin surface is produced which may come with the third application, whereas the plain oil method might require as many as five applications.

There is still another oil-combination finish that can be handled by the amateur without special skill. This is known as the shellac-oil finish, shellac being used in place of varnish mentioned above. As in the previous case, the application of this mixture is also preceded by two applications of rubbed oil.

The formula for the shellac mixture follows: $\frac{1}{3}$ of orange shellac and $\frac{2}{3}$ boiled oil. This is applied freely to the surface and rubbed until it becomes tacky and then the excess is removed with clean rags and the piece set away to dry, this procedure being repeated until satisfactory results are had. Perhaps no more than three rubbed coats will be necessary. The procedure is exactly the same as that used for varnish and oil.

This latter finish, it is to be noted, is especially suited for hard maple and oak. It is also to be noted that fillers need not be used before such finishes are applied to such woods as the better grades of mahogany, cherry, walnut, etc. The satin finish does not call for a lengthy fussing about with wood fillers because the polish desired is not excessive. Another thing: the worker should not attempt to process large surfaces at one time with the oil and varnish or the oil and shellac methods. He will find several square feet enough. In place of attempting the whole of a drop-leaf table top, he should try only the middle section first and then one leaf at a time.

It is very strange that but few amateur refinishers know how to use shellac. For one thing, they use it too thick or concentrated and for another thing most of them do not allow the eight hours necessary for it to set up to a point where steel wool or fine sandpaper may be applied to it. Yet shellac may easily be applied in such a way as to supply a very useful, beautiful and long-lived surface. It is not recommended for use, however, on furniture like tables or benches where it may come into contact with water or other liquids, especially those containing alcohol which make very short work of a shellacked surface no matter how well put on. Shellac, on the other hand, will render long service on the frames of living room chairs, picture frames and in any position indeed where it will not be exposed to hard wear or liquids of any kind.

Shellac may also be safely used over oil stains where such stains have been permitted to dry for several days. There will be no danger of the colour pigment giving any trouble.

Whether or not orange shellac is used will depend upon the colour effects desired and whether or not the shellac is to be used over oil stain. If it is to be used over a coloured surface and the worker wishes to preserve that colour as much as possible, then clear or white shellac should be used. No matter what the colour of the shellac, it is cut down considerably. Then when it is applied in the following manner, the amateur will find it within his power to produce very pleasing effects with shellac and furniture wax alone.

In no case should the shellac be used as it comes from the tin. This mixture should be used in the proportion of $\frac{1}{5}$ shellac and $\frac{4}{5}$ denatured alcohol or any of the solvent mixtures now being sold as shellac thinners.

This dilute mixture is then applied in a very thin coat, the brush being dipped sparingly so that enough shellac will not be picked up to make the stuff weep when applied to vertical surfaces. A uniform film is needed. After this is established, the shellac is permitted to dry for about eight hours. Then the surface is gone over with fine steel wool and another coat of shellac applied. This is done five or six times, the last coat being followed by the use of furniture wax after the gloss has been eliminated by the use of steel wool.

A similar process may be used on plain old pine pieces of a primitive nature. Here, however, in place of using all clear shellac or all orange shellac, one produces a honey colour by mixing the two together half and half. Then this mixture is cut with alcohol or thinner as mentioned above. Several coats will be needed.

A very pleasing antique effect may be had if about a tea-spoonful of burnt umber is mixed into the tin (ordinary size) of wax before the wax is applied. A gentle rubbing with steel wool always precedes the application of wax.

Such surfaces as the last mentioned are rather difficult to damage with anything but alcoholic liquids or excessive water. Most other marks may be quickly obliterated by an application of furniture wax and a bit of brisk rubbing.

There is a philosophy to refinishing and a knack in seeing to it that the right finish is used in the right place, not only for practical reasons but for others as well. There is the sad case of the writer's workshop pal whose wife insisted that the ladderback chairs in the dining room be finished in mahogany because friend wife had a rope-legged mahogany dining room table which she liked. One does not put walnut stain on pine deal kitchen tables or orange or clear shellac on box room furniture. Nor does one use white enamel on Empire beds or mahogany in refinishing a piece of blonde modern stuff. In the case of antique furniture, the worker will in all probability wish to preserve the old patina (colour and texture) as far as possible. This means that if the old varnish is to be removed, one must be careful not to scrape or sand-paper away any more of the old surface than necessary. It also means that clear varnish or lacquer should be used to permit the patina to show through.

There is at the present time a great deal of interest in what is known as blonde or " pickled " finishes which usually involve a rather severe bleaching of the wood before a water-white or highly transparent varnish is applied. Such finishes are used in the finishing or refinishing of modern pieces and especially the so-called modernistic styles, unfinished articles of which may now be purchased in many of the large department stores. Some such pieces are of plain maple, some carry fine veneers of the harder light-coloured woods, etc.

Even if the so-called blonde finish was desired on old pine, for instance, it would be most difficult to bring about because of the patina of the pine. This would require a heavy removal of the surface to a considerable depth and then, unless great skill was used, the scraped or hand-planed surface would be rough and uneven. Added to this would be the great damage done to old wood fibres by the use of the powerful bleach that would be necessary to use on old pine. Hence the amateur is advised to limit blonde finishes to new wood.

It is possible to purchase prepared bleaches in the larger paint stores but such paint stores are not available to many small-town readers of this book. Therefore the following formula is given for a good bleach which may be made in large supply and then bottled.

One pound of oxalic acid crystals is dissolved in warm water to produce a slightly saturated solution. Thus the crystals are added to a quart of water until it will take no more at, say, 150° Fahrenheit. Then more water is added until the crystals are all dissolved. To this mixture a pint of saturated tartaric acid solution is added.

While this bleaching solution is not extremely dangerous, it should be handled with care and respect and rubber gloves should be used when the stuff is applied. It will bleach clothing as well as wood and it will also make known its presence on skin.

The solution as mixed according to the above formula is a bit too powerful to be applied to wood. It should therefore be diluted to about half-strength by the addition of water before it is used.

Application may be made with a cotton dish mop. Such a

I

mop will last a long time if it is washed in clean, warm water after each application.

The surface to be treated is thoroughly wetted with the solution and then left to stand for about fifteen minutes, after which what remains of the solution is wiped off with clean rags (one watches out for dirty rags because the bleach will go after certain stains, dissolve them and smear them out on the freshly-treated surface) and then the worker applies several washings of clean water. The above process is repeated until a sufficiently light colour is had. To remove or neutralise the last of the bleaching solution, the worker applies a half-and-half solution of water and vinegar.

After such a treatment, the surface is permitted to dry for at least forty-eight hours in a dry place. Then it is sanded very lightly with No. 00 paper to reduce the raised grain. Water will invariably raise the grain of any wood. A water-white varnish may then be applied after the dust resulting from the sanding has been wiped away with a clean cloth dampened with turpentine.

It is also to be pointed out that this same bleaching solution is applied in the removal of stains in wood. However, one does not merely daub it on a stained spot. That might reduce or eliminate the stain but it would also leave a light-coloured blotch in a sea of darker coloured wood. The solution is applied to the whole surface and it may even be necessary to apply it to a whole article whether it needs it or not. This would be necessary if a uniform colour for prefinished wood was to be had. These are points that the amateur must bear in mind.

Aside from the foregoing there is no trick to the application of water-white varnishes needed for blonde effects. Blonde effects cannot be had, however, with bleaching and the subsequent application of ordinary lacquer or varnish with their basically amber colours.

There is also the pickled finish which may turn out to be very pleasing when used on an old piece from the late 19th to early 20th century. This finish is used only on such deeply-grained woods as oak and chestnut and may be easily achieved. However the bleaching process precedes it if the most attractive results are to be had. Some do not like pickled finishes but that is a matter of individual choice. The writer has tried to avoid supplying data for finishes that are acceptable only to his personal tastes (see Chapter 7 for Modern Finishes).

After ordinary bleaching, white paint is used to cover the oak or chestnut and this is then carefully wiped off across grain before it sets. A period of three or four hours is enough. If too long a period elapses between application and wiping, the paint is apt to become too sticky and this will produce a smeary effect. Cross-wise wiping will leave paint in the grain which is the object of the finish. A mixture of white lead and turpentine and boiled oil may also be used in place of paint with equal amounts of the latter two ingredients and just enough to produce a covering with paint-like consistency.

In any case, the paint or white lead mixture is allowed to dry thoroughly, after wiping off the excess, and then the surface is covered with a very thin (50-50) mixture of clear shellac and denatured alcohol or shellac thinner. After a few hours of drying (say seven or eight) the shellac is rubbed grain-wise with fine steel wool. Then another coat of the shellac is applied and rubbed. A light-coloured wax is then used and this is buffed with a soft cloth. The result should please those who like pickled finishes.

When finishing early 19th century chairs of the primitive types (the less fancy of the Hitchcocks for example) one should not overlook the excellent effects of the glossy enamels in dark grey, black, deep red or deep green. The writer has also seen these chairs done in buff and yellow with pleasing effects. On the other hand, some prefer to strip these chairs entirely and give them an orange shellac finish.

These chairs were made by the hundreds of thousands between 1820 and 1845 and may still be found with rush or splat bottoms. One also finds them without bottoms in the antique or second-hand shops where they may be had for between five and ten shillings each, some of them still bearing their gay striping and gay stencils on the top splat. Refinished and restencilled, such chairs may cost as much as £2 10s. each.

There is no reason why all of this work cannot be done at home. One should not be deceived by the weakness of such chairs when they do not have their bottoms in place. Bottoms lend strength and prevent wiggle. The purchaser merely sees to it that the chairs are without extensive damage such as rungs that have come loose or that have been repaired with glue (after splitting), etc.

In case of stripping and refinishing with shellac, the worker may turn the pages of this book back for instructions along this line. Any of the shellac methods previously described will be acceptable for such work, especially the method calling for a 50-50 mixture of orange and clear shellac.

If enamel is to be used, then wholesale stripping will not be necessary. In such a case, one simply sands the old finish, first with No. 0 and then No. 00 sandpaper. After this, shellac (thin) is applied and permitted to dry. This is then rubbed with fine steel wool and the new enamel applied after the chair has been wiped to free it of shellac dust.

In refinishing chairs, it will probably be wise to use two coats if weeping and the accumulation of drops on the bottom sides of the rungs is to be avoided. The first coat should barely cover. Such treatment will also help solve the dust problem because the two thin coats will set up quickly.

After the enamel is dry, it is advisable to cut the gloss with fine steel wool and then wax the surface. The result is a fine satin finish. On the other hand, if stencils are to be used or striping down the leg is to be done, the wax should be left off until the whole job is done.

Stencils are easy to handle if the beginner does not elect to go in for some of the finer effects achieved by the old masters who were hired by Hitchcock and others. Surviving craftsmen who can duplicate these stencils now can be counted on the fingers of one hand. If one wishes only to duplicate the quaint little smears that were on the top splats of some of the cheaper chairs of the Hitchcock type, there is no reason why this cannot be done by the use of stencils.

Fig. 54. Sketches at left show how parts of stencil are made separately, then applied one at a time to make figure at right.

Hitchcocks were done in plain colours, in colours with gold and bronze and in gold or bronze alone with exquisite shading effects.

If the reader wishes to experiment with the latter, he may proceed as follows: First a few experimental panels of ply-wood are made and covered with the enamel to be used on the chairs. (Bronze and gold were usually used on black or deep green chairs.) Then some suitable design is copied either from an actual chair or from a book devoted to antiques. These stencils were never made in one piece. Some of them (see Fig. 54) had eight or ten pieces. For example, when a compote was used (a popular design in the old days) there was a stencil for this and a stencil for each one of the fruits in the compote, such as peaches, cherries, apples, grapes, melons, etc. Each stencil was put in place and used separately, starting with the compote.

The oiled paper used by painters for cutting stencils may be had from any large paint shop. A very thin grade should be had, the thinner the paper the sharper the outline of the stencil. The design is transferred to this and cut with a razor blade. If such oiled paper is not available, wrapping paper soaked with molten paraffin wax may be used.

The worker will also have to make himself what is known as a pounce bag. This amounts merely to a clean piece of velvet in which a little sand is wrapped tightly, the velvet being tied at the top in the manner of a bag. This bag is used to pick up the different gold or bronze powders of which only the best grades should be purchased. With these simple preparations, the worker will be ready to set about applying stencils to his experimental panels.

Next, he applies a thin coat of spar varnish to a panel and permits it to set several hours until it reaches a tacky state. He then puts his first stencil in place and presses the pounce bag gently into a bit of the bronze or gold powder. This is then gently applied to the tacky surface of varnish within the stencil opening.

One of the most difficult things to control in the application of the powder is the powder itself, which is very light and fluffy and is easily blown about even by one's breath. When it is blown about it is apt to settle where it is not wanted, thereby flecking the work badly.

Preventive measures amount to working in a draughtless, closed room, wearing a handkerchief over the nose to control the breath, and not picking up more powder than is needed with the pounce bag. One of the most deadly of the dangers is the powder that will flutter down upon the tacky and clean surface underneath the stencil at the time the stencil is lifted. This amounts to excess powder left on the fringes of the stencil design when the pounce bag is used. To avoid such disasters, the worker is warned to carefully wipe this excess powder away with a damp cloth over the end of a finger before he attempts to lift the stencil, which must be done before the varnish sets up underneath it.

Perhaps by the time he has used up five or more of the experimental panels, the worker will feel that he has gained enough confidence and skill to proceed with his first chair. If the effort is successful, the chair is set away to dry after the last piece of the stencil has been used. Then after the stencil varnish has set up, varnish is applied over the whole stencil to protect it. After this has dried hard, the whole chair (including the stencil) may be gone over with fine steel wool which is followed by wax.

Many of the less costly chairs of the Hitchcock type were hand-painted with flower and fruit designs. However, one has to be very clever with a brush to duplicate these quaint little floral groups, although the trick can be turned by the use of stencils if the worker has had a chance to trace over the painting on such a chair, using a soft pencil and tissue paper as the first step in preparing a stencil. After the stencil has been used, a brush may be employed to paint in the disconnected parts left by the stencil, thereby producing what is to all intents and purposes a painting rather than a stencil.

Ordinarily colour enamels cannot be used for this purpose. One uses a home-made mixture for this work. Made-to-order preparations as sold in the stores are far too liquid for the work at hand and would seep in beneath the stencil edges. It is best by far that the worker prepare his own mixtures as follows:

A small tin of flat white is purchased and a part (about $\frac{1}{2}$) of the unmixed oils on the top is poured off and set aside. This will leave a pretty thick mixture after it is stirred up. It is this thick mixture that the worker colours (a small amount for each colour) for use in painting the designs on the chair splats.

If, for instance, red, green and yellow are to be used in the design, a small tube of each one of these ground colours is purchased at the paint shop or even at an art shop for ordinary oil colours used by artists will serve. To two or three tablespoons of the basic white mixture, the worker adds one of the colours he is using until the proper shade is had.

Such a coloured mixture will dry out pretty dull but little trouble will be had by running and unwanted blending will also be more easily avoided if one waits an hour or two before applying another colour. The dull cast after drying is corrected by an application of a good spar or other varnish over the whole splat of the chair. This will give the design a desirable gloss; perhaps too much. In that event, the gloss of the varnish is cut with fine steel wool and furniture wax is applied.

While speaking of stencils and old paintings on the splats of the so-called " fancy " chairs, it is well to recall that many of these are found in excellent condition save for the fact that they lie buried under several applications of old varnish. This is not only true of chairs but also stencilled chest fronts, clock and mirror pilasters and a few beds of the 1820-1830 era. During the late 1820s and up to the late 1830s, much of the furniture for use by the growing middle class and the more wealthy of the farmers was so decorated. It permitted these people to ape the elegance of the more well-to-do folk in the urban centres.

Such stencils may often be rescued from beneath old varnish if a little patience is shown by the operator. He simply arms himself with the resolve not to rush, a few clean rags, a brush and a tin of good commercial varnish remover. Thin layers of the latter are applied and the softened varnish wiped away quickly. Here one seeks to prevent a too-deep penetration of the remover in an effort to protect the design. Therefore a large number of thin applications are recommended, applications that should not be permitted to stand nearly so long as the directions on the tin or bottle state. Also the worker should be careful not to carry the removal to the actual surface of the stencil. He should stop short of this, leaving a thin layer of old varnish which may be carefully brushed away with fine steel wool after the varnish has set up again. One will be able to tell of the approach to the stencil by the increasing brightness as the old varnish is wiped away.

A quick test for the uniformity of the varnish removal after the steel wool is applied may be had by wiping the surface of the stencil with a mixture of 25 per cent boiled oil and 75 per cent turpentine. This will instantly brighten the stencil and permit the worker to locate spots in need of additional varnish removal.

This whole business of finishing and refinishing is a complicated one if the beginner reads too much of the various authorities who do not always agree. Further to confuse the beginner are the many rather silly claims made by the manufacturers of new and synthetic products, some of which are rather over-rated. The true value of finishes is not determined over-night or by a few acceleration tests in a laboratory. Hence the reader is cautioned to remain pretty close to the shore of traditional practice save in the case of the proven lacquers. The writer has tried to deal only with things that beginners can handle with assurance and with finishes that have the greatest possible promise of remaining beautiful and serviceable over a period of years.

One of the most annoying problems met up with by the amateur refinisher is that of matching a new piece of wood with an old piece where a repair has been made. The case of an old cherry table may be cited where a new leaf has replaced an old one. Old cherry is always deep reddish-brown while a new piece may have streaks of light brown running through areas of medium reddish brown. Unless some colouring is done on the new wood, a very disappointing match will be had. Of course the best answer to this problem is to replace the old leaf with a piece of old cherry. Then no matching will be required. Hence the advice never to miss a chance to purchase old cherry chests, tables, etc., at country auctions, even though the pieces purchased are not in good condition, should not be forgotten. The wood is invaluable. The same advice can, of course, be followed in the case of old pine, walnut and maple whether plain, buckhorn, striped or curly.

The matter of matching old with new cherry is not too difficult nor is the problem solved by merely covering the new cherry with a prepared oil stain of that colour. Rather the worker will have to mix his own stuff and it should be much darker in colour than any of the ready-to-use cherry stains.

To a mixture of three parts of boiled linseed oil, one part turpentine and one-half part japan drier, the workman adds Italian burnt sienna until the proper depth is had. The mixture is stirred for some time before it is used and it is better to err on the light side than on the dark. A light surface can always be made darker but it is difficult to make a dark surface lighter in colour. The burnt sienna mentioned above is already mixed with oil when it is purchased in small collapsible tubes. One should permit the freshly applied cherry stain to dry before the decision as to colour match is made.

The nice thing about these home-made oil stains is that they may be used for matching old with new wood because the worker may make them as light or dark as he pleases. Old wood, of any kind, is always darker than new wood.

In case the worker wishes to mix up his own oil stains for matching purposes, the basic formula for the linseed-oil-drier-turpentine mixture is always the same for any colour. The oil colours mixed into this to produce the various wood colours in light or deep shades follow:

WALNUT
    Four parts Turkey burnt umber
    One part Vandyke brown

LIGHT CHERRY
    Two parts of Italian raw sienna
    Three parts of Italian burnt sienna

BROWN MAHOGANY
    Three parts Italian burnt sienna
    One part rose pink or maroon lake
    One part Vandyke brown

RED MAHOGANY
    Three parts Italian burnt sienna
    Two parts rose pink

DARK CHERRY
    Italian burnt sienna

DARK OAK
    One part Turkey burnt umber
    Four parts Italian raw sienna

In all cases where the worker is seeking to match old with new wood, he makes the first application of the colour light. The above formulas may be made lighter or darker as needs dictate.

One of the most difficult matches to bring about is one between old and new pine. The colour and patina of the old pine will depend in a very large measure upon whether it has ever been painted, whether it has been waxed, whether it has been shellacked, etc. No set rule can be made as to what mixture goes into what for such a match. If the old pine to be matched has never had any preparation on its surface, a match brought about with oil colours of the type just described is out. Such colours will set up with a mild sheen whereas old pine that has never been refinished is very dull. On the other hand, if the sheen left by the oil colour is removed with sandpaper, the shade of the colour will change.

One thing is fortunate: the workman can have at his disposal any amount of new pine so that he may try any number of matches before he decides upon the proper one. In each case, he permits the experimental colour to dry before he decides whether or not the correct colour is at hand.

The best material to employ in bringing about a match between old and new wood (pine included) is water stain, the colouring matter being supplied by the acid coal-tar range of colours in all large paint stores and in a large range of colours and shades. What is sought by the worker in the case of matching old pine that was never before painted or varnished is a coffee-coloured stain and this information should be passed on to the paint store clerk. Old pine is about as close in colour to a coffee stain on a white tablecloth as anything that can be imagined. It is to be remembered that these acid coal-tar dyes when mixed with water have a terrific covering power. Hence very little basic material will be needed.

After the stuff has been dissolved in water, the mixture is tried for colour on an experimental block of pine. This procedure is followed until the perfect match is had in the dry state.

The end grain of pine, or any other wood for that matter, has an insatiable appetite for all of the spirit, water and oil stains. If the worker applies his water stain to the raw, open end grain, it will sponge it up rapidly and dry out many shades darker than the other surface. In fact, it will provide a band of mourning. Therefore in the case of applying water stains this end grain is sponged with clean water first and after this has had a chance to soak in, the water stain is applied. After a minute or two, part of this is wiped away to prevent too much of it from being absorbed deep into the end grain. Here again, it is better to have it too light than too dark. Another application will take care of a surface that is too light.

It is true that these water stains raise the grain of the wood to a very pronounced degree but in the present instance, where no polished or semi-polished finish is desired, this is not an important consideration. After drying, the raised grain will in some measure shrink back. Where a polished or varnished surface is to be had over such stains, sanding with No. 000 sandpaper is necessary after the water stain is thoroughly dry.

By and large this colour-matching business is tricky, often stumping old experienced workers and the beginner's only protection against disastrous mistakes is to work slowly and make sure of the *dry* colour he will get by employing sample blocks or working on the underside of pieces already a part of the furniture he is refinishing. No book instruction can cover the subject perfectly, due to the many factors.

Colour varnishes or varnish stains amount to varnish in which the staining materials are already mixed and such things are handled in exactly the same manner as clear varnish. The principal colours are red and brown mahogany, oak and walnut in various shades. Two coats are usually recommended by the manufacturer with sanding down between the first and second coats. If the high gloss left by the second coat is found objectionable, a light treatment with steel wool and wax will relieve this with very little trouble.

Such varnishes may or may not be applied over filled

surfaces, depending upon the grain of the wood. In cases where the colour might be too dark, some manufacturers supply an undercoating material which is permitted to dry for twenty-four hours before the colour varnish is put in place.

It would appear, as far as the amateur is concerned at least, that he has better control over the ultimate colour of his work by using oil stain and clear varnish rather than colour varnish where the shade supplied by the manufactured material is difficult to alter. Certainly the beginner is strongly advised against mixing new material into standard formulas or diluting them without knowing what he is doing.

THE MODERN FINISHES

There are a number of modern finishes that are especially useful in producing "that new look" on functional furniture. These finishes are also practical and in most cases they may be very easily produced.

In the finish about to be outlined, the application of lacquer is preceded by use of bleach, either the type previously described or, in case extreme bleached effects are desired, one of the powerful bleaching mixtures now sold in the large paint stores. These are applied with a rubber sponge and the worker should use rubber gloves to protect his hands. Most of the powerful new bleaches have hydrogen peroxide in them and no harmful residue is to be found after the bleaching process.

If the worker wishes to check results of these bleaches before he goes "all out," it might be advisable to try the solutions either on test panels or on the underside of the furniture to be finished. It may be said that the results are apt to be disappointing when the finish about to be described is tried on dark walnut or other dark woods. On the other hand, excellent results may be anticipated when this finish is applied to such woods as maple, birch, chestnut, oak, etc. Pine does not have enough grain character, however, for finishes of this type.

After the wood has thoroughly recovered from the application of the bleach and is completely dry, a mixture of *white* and *clear* lacquer is put on. This mixture is made by adding one part of white lacquer to four parts of clear lacquer. Whether the mixture is sprayed or brushed on the surface, it should be greatly thinned (50-50) before use. In any case, the wood upon which such a preparation is placed will be greatly lightened and the general effect is apt to be very pleasing. A second or even a third thin coat will not greatly alter the original appearance. It might be mentioned that this is often the finish one sees in many of the smart modernistic shops nowadays. The process itself is referred to as " toning " by modern finishers.

What has become known to the trade as honeytoned maple is also delightful to behold and lies easily within the range of the amateur to produce. White birch may also be treated in the manner reviewed below. To achieve this, the worker simply sands the wood without bleaching it and applies the white and clear lacquer mixture recommended in the previous finish. Over this, two thin coats of water-white lacquer are brushed or sprayed. When these lacquer finishes are brushed on, it may be advisable to use fine waterproof sandpaper between coats.

The so-called honeytone effect may also be had on the above-mentioned woods by the use of the bleaching solution and only the water-white lacquer which is applied in two or more coats. In this case, the white-clear lacquer mixture is left out.

What has become known as limed oak is also finding wide approval these days. To produce this, the oak is first bleached and then covered with a wash coat of water-white lacquer. Such wash coats are very thin and call for a 1-10 mixture (1 part lacquer, 10 parts thinner) of the water-white lacquer and the thinner. After this has dried, the surface is brushed over with a thinned-out mixture with the consistency of paint, composed of zinc-white oil colour and natural colour filler. After this has thoroughly dried, one or two applications of water-white lacquer is put on. The end effect should be pleasing.

What has become known as silvered oak is similar to limed oak although the treatment is quite different. In this case, bleaching is followed by the application of a mixture made up of one part of light or pearl grey lacquer and three parts of clear lacquer. One coat of this will be sufficient and after this has dried, the pores of the grain are filled with white filler thinned out to fluid form. Excess is brushed away with a clean rag moving across the grain. After the latter is absolutely dry and hard, a finishing of two or three thin coats of water-white lacquer is applied after very light sanding.

There is also the bone-white lacquer finish which is produced in the following manner: Inasmuch as this is not a transparent finish, the use of bleach will not be necessary. The worker seeks only a clean, smooth surface. A wash coat of very thin water-white or clear lacquer followed by sanding with No. 000 sandpaper may supply a better base. This is, however, optional.

Bone-white lacquer which is just off-white shade, may be had already mixed or the worker may produce it himself by adding a touch of brown to white lacquer. The amount of added brown will depend upon the shade desired, but let the mixer beware of the great sensitivity of white lacquer, paint or enamel to the presence of other colours. A few teaspoonfuls of brown to a quart will usually do the trick. Complete stirring must be had before the final colour can be determined.

The application of bone-white lacquer is followed by a brushed-on application of a medium brown wiping stain which is wiped away before it has a chance to set up. Here the worker may exercise his artistic talents by producing a nice shading effect. These wiping stains are merely concentrated pigment stains.

K

After the complete drying of the wiping stain, for which at least two days should be allowed, the article is covered with two or more coats of clear lacquer.

This application of a wiping stain and its subsequent removal with a rag is called high-lighting by the trade. Some extremely interesting effects may be obtained with it without a great deal of skill. Perhaps some readers have stopped to admire the " antique maple " effects seen on furniture in the store windows. Such effects are obtained by this high-lighting process. Although such effects are obtained in many different ways, the easiest is that of applying the proper shade of wiping stain and removing most of it. Of course, to wipe the stain away evenly and to leave a uniform colour behind would be stupid. On a turned leg, for example, the worker wipes from end to end and makes little attempt to completely remove the stain from grooves. He brushes the rag over the surface in such a manner that only the highest spots are touched. The result is a fine shading. On a panelled cabinet door, he brushes the centre clean and leaves the edges with very little or no wiping at all bleeding off gradually to the edges. If, in the case of " antiqued " maple, a light enough wiping stain has been used, the effect will be perfect. Some practice panels for use with high-lighting will help.

This antique maple effect is produced in the manner described below. In the case of all of these modern finishes it is assumed that fresh, new wood is used. The writer cannot endorse such finishes when it is planned to use them on old wood which may be deeply coloured because of age.

The maple or other wood to be finished is first given a coat of red-orange wiping stain. If an error is to be made on the length of time the stain is permitted to remain before it is wiped away, let the error be on the side of too little rather than too much time. As in all cases, a surface that turns out to be too light can be easily remedied, whereas a too-dark surface is a problem indeed. In this first coat of stain, one seeks to produce an even colour. High-lighting will follow.

After this stain is completely dry, for which two days should be allowed, the surface should be gone over with a thin coat of clear lacquer. After this has dried, a second coat of wiping stain is placed over the lacquer and the high-lighting is produced with this. A medium brown stain is used to produce the high-lighting.

When this second application of stain is absolutely dry, the worker proceeds to apply a protective coat of clear lacquer, or even clear varnish if he wishes, remembering that varnish can be placed over lacquer but not lacquer over varnish.

So far in discussing these modern finishes, no mention has been made of mahogany and little mention has been made of walnut save to warn the worker away from it. There are, however, certain modern treatments that may be applied to such woods with pleasing effects.

There is what is known as the " heather " finish for mahogany, the end effects of which vary somewhat with the type of mahogany and its place of growth, Honduras, Cuba, San Domingo, etc. In the one case, the mahogany, most of which is a very grainy wood, is filled with a relatively thin mixture of white filler. The excess is wiped away across grain. A very light sanding with No. 000 sandpaper may be advisable after this, working with the grain. An application of two coats of water-white lacquer or varnish follows after long drying.

Another delightful effect referred to in the trade as " tweed " is produced in the manner above, the only change being that of adding a small amount of red colour to the natural filler used. This gives a pleasant pink tone.

There are some professional workers who, in some cases, apply a bleach to mahogany and then follow this with a natural coloured filler. This is in turn followed with a diluted stain, the colour of which may suit the worker's fancy. Some test panels will reveal the effect most desired. Final covering with water-white lacquer or varnish is recommended.

The same finishes as outlined for mahogany may also be used on walnut if the worker wishes, the final tone varying to some degree. What is known as amber walnut is produced by applying bleach and following this with amber stain. A sealer coat of thin lacquer is then followed by very thin natural filler with a final coat of clear lacquer.

There is still another finish for walnut called " old world." To produce this, the worker first bleaches the wood, using one of the powerful modern preparations. After a seal is produced with a wash coat of very thin clear lacquer, a natural filler tinted with burnt umber is put on. This burnt umber is mixed with oil before being blended with the filler. The depth of tone of this mixture should not be too deep. Much will depend upon the tastes of the worker. Usually a light shade is most desired because shading with a brown wiping stain follows. Finish is produced with clear lacquer or varnish.

The colour enamels so often used on the unfinished furniture now available are apt to be a bit harsh unless some care is used in their application.   Rare indeed is the impatient amateur who is willing to devote the time needed to produce a good effect.   When applied without proper care and technique, such enamels shine to the point of glare and no well-finished article of furniture should produce a glare in any kind of light.

Of course, the matter of sanding is important. This is followed *always* by a bottom or priming coat of flat white, preferably made by the manufacturer of the enamel that is to be used. After it is dry, the priming coat is carefully sanded smooth with No. 00 sandpaper. All dust from this operation is removed with a cloth moistened in clean turpentine.

Unlike paint, enamel should not be brushed out too much and considerable material should be carried to the work from the tin. Brushing out should stop just beyond the point where weeping might be produced on a vertical surface. If at all possible, vertical surfaces should be placed in a horizontal position while being covered.

After the first coat of enamel is set up and perfectly dry, it should be sanded slightly with No. 00 paper and all dust from the operation again removed before the second and last coat is applied. This second coat is rubbed gently with pumice and crude oil which is followed by an application of furniture wax after the surface has been washed with soft soap and water. The result is a smooth, semi-gloss finish very pleasing to the eye.

If in producing such finishes, the worker wishes to stripe the bulbous turnings on the legs of chairs or tables, let him not forget the convenience of using masking tape for this purpose. Such tape comes in rolls of various widths and, like Scotch type, may be pulled from the surface to which it adheres with no danger of a deposit being left.

For instance, one might wish to stripe a contrasting colour band around the top of a kitchen table near its edge. Anyone but a sign or coach painter with a special striping brush will find this a difficult job.

With the use of masking tape, this operation may be conducted with every assurance of complete and satisfying success worthy of a professional. If two parallel strips of tape are laid with the intervening space representing the width of the stripe desired, one simply has to apply the enamel to this space and wait for it to dry. After the tape is removed, the margin of the stripe will be clean and sharp.

Small, simple designs may be worked out by the use of such tape. If one cares to spend the time necessary, complicated stencil effects may also be worked out. To do this, the worker simply lays two or more (depending upon the width of the tape and of the design proposed) strips of the tape side by side. One takes care to see that in laying the tape, it is pressed down tight and the edges made to butt perfectly to prevent paint seepage later.

The design may be made on a separate piece of paper and then transferred to the masking tape. It is then cut out with one of the new thin-bladed knives used by the model-making fraternity. In general, stencils produced in this manner are much sharper in outline than those produced by the use of regular stencil paper. This is because of the lack of paint or enamel seepage under the edges of the tape which are sealed tight against the surface being worked upon. Of course, one of the difficulties of using such stencils when they are made up of several lengths of tape lying side by side is the care needed to lift the strips of tape and re-lay them properly in repeating the stencil. It can, however, be done by a careful worker. In every case, the tape is permitted to remain in position until the enamel used is at least semi-dry.

During the past few years, the difficulty of buying good new furniture and the high cost of such furniture when available has forced many young married folk into the second-hand market. Many clever young people have therefore discovered the charming effects that may be had by working over the finishes of old pieces with white, cream or buff enamels and treating these surfaces with gay stencils or hand-painted floral or fruit pictures. In case the young folk do not have the artistic talent needed for the latter, there is always the stencil which practically guarantees a professional job.

It is commonly conceded that the mission and golden oak furniture of the 1890-1910 period was monstrous from an artistic standpoint, but has the imaginative reader contemplated the miracles that may be wrought with such furniture by simple refinishing methods using either modern coloured lacquers or enamels? From a purely utilitarian viewpoint, such furniture is just as good to-day as it was the day it was made unless, of course, it has suffered extensive physical damage. This is also the case of the stark and very awkward late Victorian commodes which may be had in the secondhand store for 5s. or so. They are indeed gawky things with shallow carving and little bottom compartments reserved for the chamber mug. Within a few hours' time, however, they may sally forth from the basement workshop gay and happy to take their place in a bedroom. The same for beds, tables, chairs, etc.

If one plans on the use of enamels over such pieces of furniture, it is necessary only to lightly sand the surface of the old finish (it is usually original in these pieces) before the enamel is applied. Stripping is not necessary. However, if lacquer is to be applied, it must be remembered that the solvents will soften the varnish underneath and permit it to bleed through. Enamels would therefore appear more sensible to use in work of this nature, unless one wishes to go to the trouble of removing old finishes.

A short time before the material for this book was assembled, two young friends of the writer purchased a battered cedar blanket chest for which they paid 10s. Within a week's time they had it charmingly transformed into a stencilled early Dutch hope chest for which they were subsequently offered £10.

In applying such stencils one should use only approved stencil paper, stencil brushes and enamel that is not so thin as to increase the danger of its seeping under the edges of the stencil paper. Such paper may be purchased at paint stores, but, if it is not available in a small town, there is no reason why the worker cannot prepare his own by immersing a good tough wrapping paper in molten wax.

It has been pointed out before that a separate stencil should usually be made for each colour to be applied. Each application of enamel should also be permitted to dry smear-proof before another is applied.

RE-UPHOLSTERING

Male experience with the problem of re-upholstering makes it advisable at the very outset to call in friend wife for assistance. For one thing, she has what might be called a " cloth sense " and she also has fingers that are not all thumbs when it comes to sewing. Brave indeed is the home workman who sets out alone to conquer such jobs. The crude mechanical work is not difficult but the work with the needle and thread may be.

The first decision to be made is whether a chair is simply in need of recovering or a complete job of re-upholstering, which means stripping it to the frame and starting from scratch. The age of a chair or other piece is important here. If the chair is an old thing (say fifty years) and it still has a good shape because of careful use, the chances are that the inner materials, like the webbing, twine and burlap, will be pretty well dried out and unable to survive normal usage for any great length of time. One may therefore go to the trouble of replacing the covering only to find that the insides give up the battle a few months later. Therefore, even though such chairs have retained their shapes, it is best to replace the whole works while one is at it.

On the other hand, if a chair is relatively new and is well preserved in form, never having been recovered before, the chances are that its innards will bear up for some time to come. In such cases a mere recovering may do. Much depends upon the original cost of the chair. The worker will have to use his best judgment in such matters remembering that it is a most disheartening situation to recover a chair with good material only to discover a few months later that the springs have shifted or that sagging develops because of stretched or broken webbing, etc.

Simple recovering will be treated first. That does not mean that the worker should go after a chair with a sharp knife or scissors and strip it without regard for the pattern. An expert does not always need a pattern but beginners must have one and there is only one way to get it—by careful removal of the old material. Each tack is removed carefully and each stitch, if need be, is carefully ripped with an old safety razor blade. After all of the pieces have been removed, they are placed in a row on the floor as close together as possible. Here the worker discovers how many yards of material will be needed for recovering. Measurement is accomplished with a yardstick and it will be necessary to gauge the yardage based on material widths of either 26 or 54 inches. It is best to go to the shop armed with figures of yardage needed for both widths. It may be that the material of choice comes only in one of the widths. Cutting down waste is important.

The first matter treated will be that of simply recovering chairs. A description of the full stem-to-stern job will be given later.

Of course, the simplest of all jobs is that of recovering slip seats of side chairs, the slip seat being padded and without springs of any sort. These seats are usually held from beneath with four corner screws and after the removal of these, the seat is free. The covering material is merely lapped over the edges and held with tacks to a wooden bottom. It might be well to remove and use the first piece of material as a pattern if more than one of a set of matching chairs is to be treated. Between the covering material and the padding there is a piece of muslin and if the padding should be badly sunken, this muslin should also be removed and, if in good shape, it may be saved and replaced (see Fig. 55).

Badly packed padding should be entirely removed and pulled apart completely and if need be some fresh material may be added to it, especially in the centre which carries most of the weight. All lumps should be worked out. This done and the padding carefully placed in position, the muslin is also placed back in position and re-tacked. If the tacks are driven in too hard, they will pierce the material and cause it to tear later. The same holds for the top material.

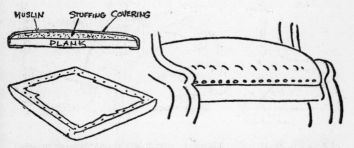

FIGS. 55 and 56. At left, the method used in recovering slip seat from dining room or occasional chair. Note that muslin is placed between stuffing and outer covering. Occasional chairs without slip seats (right) usually have the covering material held as shown with exposed brass tacks or regular tacks covered with gimp.

In the case of a side chair of the type shown in Fig. 56 where brass tacks are used on the front of the chair, the procedure is the same as above save for the replacing of the tacks. Such tacks should be purchased new because the old ones will be bent by removal and their heads may not withstand a second driving. Again driving should not be so tight as to run the risk of the tack heads cutting through the material. Straight driving is also needed. If a tack starts badly, it should be withdrawn and re-started.

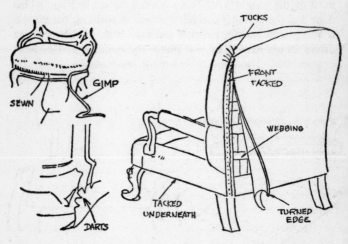

FIGS. 57, 58 and 59. Sketch at upper left shows how sewn seam of Victorian side chair is covered with gimp. At lower left note how darts are cut to work covering material around the back post of a Victorian side chair. Right, how the back covering of a Cogswell chair is put in place. Note that the edge is turned in all the way around. Small gimp tacks may be used for back covering.

Tacks merely driven back into the old holes may not remain in place. Hence the old holes should be avoided. Filling them with plastic wood will not help for this material is very hard and brittle after it sets up. It is best to place the new tacks so that they will come in between the old holes.

The sort of Victorian chair shown in Fig. 57 is a bit more difficult to handle because the raw edges of the covering come down over the seat on the outside of the seat frame and must be covered with gimp and tiny gimp tacks. The covering material is put in place and tacked in the usual manner. Tacking may start at the rear. The material is then pulled forward tightly and the front tacks put in place, avoiding all wrinkles. The edge of the new material is shirred with hemp thread.

Some prefer to glue gimp in place rather than tack it. In such a case a good quality of glue (old fashioned) is used and the gimp may be set with pins while the glue is drying. Where the covering material is to be set around the back supports on such a chair, darts may be cut out as shown in Fig. 58. The back of the chair is treated in the same manner. Such chairs, however, are equipped with springs and the above procedure presupposes that only a covering and not a whole new upholstery job is required. An upholstering job well done will usually outlast two coverings in an average well-regulated household where the children are not permitted to use chairs as work tables or diving platforms. The cambric dust catchers underneath chairs are usually tacked in place although glue may be used.

If the man-and-wife team can muster enough courage, there is no reason why they should not tackle a larger job like that of recovering a Cogswell chair as an example, assuming that the upholstering is in fair shape and looks as though it could outlast another face lifting. After all, patience is the largest asset one needs in such work. The final tacking can always wait until the workers are perfectly satisfied with fit, etc. Nothing that will be done cannot be re-done if the work is not satisfactory. In these days of high costs, many hard-earned pounds may be saved by turning the space in the basement into a busy shop.

The following may sound a great deal more precautionary than practice proves it to be. Before a piece of material is removed from a Cogswell or any chair having the more elaborate forms of upholstery, friend wife and her more awkward helper should take a pad and pencil and go over the chair, noting carefully all of the details and making simple sketches of parts where the memory might not be trusted. It will be too late after the chair has been denuded. Also, as in all cases, the old material is removed with care to preserve it for patterns. The manner in which the material is fitted to the seat of a Cogswell chair is especially important.

Assuming that the old material has been removed and the new material is cut to size and ready for application, it is best that the new covering on the front of the chair back is put in place first. This is tacked at the bottom and carried up over the back of the chair and tacked to the frame on the pads. Perhaps it will be wise to experiment with the corner tucks before a single tack is driven home in this vicinity. After the worker (here the deft fingers of friend wife may be required) is satisfied that he (or she) can make even, well-proportioned tucks, tacking, one tack for each tuck, may proceed. The rest of the tacks may be placed about one inch apart. Too many tacks only add to the difficulties of replacing material later.

The back covering piece is put in place next and this is a patching job which covers up all of the raw edges of the front cover piece. Naturally great care should be taken in cutting this material so that the fit will be accurate with enough allowance so that the edges may be folded under. Tacking may be done with gimp tacks (very small) or with the smaller size brass-topped upholstery tacks.

There is nothing difficult about the seat frame if the workers have taken care to note the manner of installation before the old material was removed. As seen in Fig. 59

the side piece of the seat frame covering comes to the back of the chair and is covered by the back piece.

The arm pad covering may be installed before or after the front of the back of the chair is put in place. Some prefer to make the installation of the arm pad covering before the front of the back is covered, in order that the latter covering may be set so as to cover the inner end of the pad covering. The other end of the pad covering is naturally turned under and it will be necessary to turn the chair upside down in tacking the arm pad material to the bottom side of the arms.

Again the worker is strongly advised to carefully examine each job before he removes any material. He should note whether parts are glued, sewn or tacked, how folds and tucks are made, corners turned, etc. Also one should tack or pin material temporarily until all wrinkles and bulges have been removed. Fussing for a half-hour or so is often necessary before one proceeds with the final tacking. Material should never be pulled so tightly that tacks may not hold it in place for a long time. Such extreme pulling is very apt to cause serious stretching of the material and tearing at the point of tacking.

The procedures to be followed in the case of a large wing chair are shown in Fig. 60. Here the workers again start with the front of the back. After smoothing the material out and making sure that the overhanging edge at the top is uniform, this edge is then tacked to the back of the top of the chair frame. Ordinary tacks are used inasmuch as this tacked edge will later be covered. Tacking is started in the centre (always), the worker moving first to one end and then to the other checking his smoothness as he moves along. In the present case, plenty of material is used in the cover for the front of the back because of the tuck-in for the sides and seat.

The next job requires friend wife at the sewing machine where the two sides of the wing segments must be sewn together at the edges with the welting fringe sewn between. This would be far too tricky for the average man and he is advised to shy away from it.

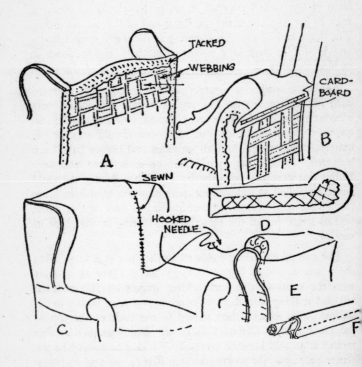

FIG. 60. (A) Method of installing webbing. (B) How a cardboard strip is used to start the side covering. (C) The method of sewing the wing covering to the back of a wing chair. (D) Back of the cardboard covering for the arm front and the stitches used to hold the covering material in place. This piece is first pinned in place as shown at E. (F) How welting is made.

These wing sections should be made to smooth out before they are finally put in place. Once in place satisfactorily, they are basted to the side sections of the chair's back cover and tucked into the groove. A curved upholsterer's needle is used to sew these pieces into the hidden parts of the groove. This will not be difficult with such a needle, using heavy thread for the purpose. If the worker uses plenty of pins as temporary holdings during such an operation, little trouble will be had. The trouble with most amateur re-upholsterers is that they proceed to tack or sew before a decent fit has been established or all of the wrinkles have been pulled out.

The front section of the chair covering (lower part, that is) comes up, after being tacked on the under edge of the frame, and is folded under the seat cushion where its end is sewed to the denim. A neat job requires that the raw edge be folded under first. It may help in this sewing if the first preliminary or holding stitches are taken with a curved upholsterer's needle. The opposite end of this front piece is carried underneath the front of the chair and tacked to the inside of the frame. This is done, however, only after the upper edge has been sewn to the denim bottom. It is much easier to pull fabric tight and tack it than pull it tight and sew it.

The arms of a wing chair may be covered easily enough with the following instructions. The inside sections are done first. After making sure of the fit, the worker proceeds to curve the material over the front edges (Fig. 60-B) of the arms and tack it at intervals of an inch or so. The upper edge is rolled under the arm and tacked.

It will be noted from Fig. 60 that the arm covering is made with three separate pieces of material. There is the inside, the outside and the front. This outside piece is put in place as illustrated in Fig. 60-B. It will be noticed that a heavy cardboard strip about one inch wide is used in connection with the side piece. This is tacked to the chair frame in the manner shown and then the side piece is folded over it and carried to the inside bottom of the frame where the final tacking is done. This leaves the cardboard strip covered and the strip in turn provides the upper edge of the side covering with a clean, smooth edge.

Two identical cardboard pieces of the shape shown at Fig. 60-D, one for the right arm front and one for the left, are cut. Both of these are covered with fabric and held in place with catch-stitching as shown in Fig. 60-D. The worker makes sure here that the covering is put on so it will be face out when the time comes for tacking the piece in place on the chair arm. Welting is sewn around the edges of both of these pieces after they have been covered. Gimp tacks are used for fastening the covered cardboard pieces to the arm fronts. If these tacks are used close to the welt, even pushing the welt over a bit as the tack is driven in, there is no reason why the tacks should show.

If more than mere re-covering is needed, the amateur will have to discover some of the methods used in complete re-upholstering. This involves the practice used in mounting and tying coiled springs, the installation of webbing, etc.

Here a word to the wise may help. One should not attempt to merely repair very old upholstery although the temptation may be great. After a chair, couch or sofa has been re-covered, it is indeed maddening to find that shortly afterward the springs break or lose their anchorage and that a large part of the whole job must be torn out and done over again. The webbing, fabric and twine used in upholstery dry out and lose strength. Hence even though a chair that was upholstered fifty years ago needs but a spring or two replaced, or re-tied, such repairs very soon have to be followed by others. There-fore it is best that the whole innards be ripped out while one is at it. Both time and money will be saved. Another thing:

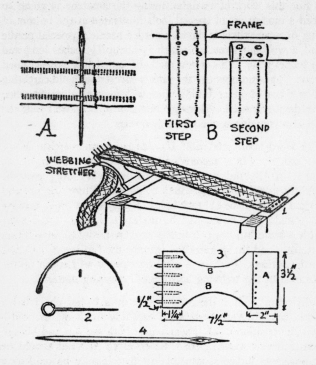

Fig. 61. (A) The method of making a temporary splice in webbing.
(B) The proper method of tacking webbing to chair frame. Centre
sketch shows how the webbing stretcher is used and at bottom may
be seen details of the construction of a stretcher. Also illustrated
are needles and pins (with loop) used by upholsterers.

the beginner will learn much about re-upholstering, perhaps
even more than this book can teach him, if he will tear out
upholstery slowly and carefully study its method of installation as he moves along.

For this work of re-upholstering the amateur is going to need a modest set of special tools illustrated at the bottom of Fig. 61 where there is shown a curved needle, a special needle and a webbing stretcher which is about $7\frac{1}{2}$ inches long and $3\frac{1}{2}$ inches wide. This is best made of some hard, close-grained wood. The end opposite the pins is covered with old carpeting or a piece of inner tubing that will prevent slipping when the device is used. Although not shown, it is well that the kit also contains a good tack hammer.

A word about material: If a chair or other article is not too old, then it is recommended that the worker re-use as much of the old material as possible. Webbing may be slightly stretched but that may be pulled up more tightly and tacked to avoid the old tack holes. Rarely will a broken spring be found. The twine will be useless and may be cut away with a knife but not before the worker studies its installation carefully and investigates the manner used in tying the knots to the springs. Perhaps a good tack puller will speed up the removal of the webbing and the old covering material.

In event such a thing as a sofa or a barrel chair has a piped back, the worker should carefully mark off the width and the position of each segment at both the top and bottom before it is removed. Also the covering material should be removed as intact as possible so that it may be used as a pattern. It is also well to place this old material over the new and to mark off the width and the position of each one of the rolls or the pipe.

Once a chair or sofa has been stripped, it is best to carefully examine the frame joints before the work of re-upholstering is begun. It may be that a corner block or two is needed and that is certainly the time to install such things.

In a moderately new piece of furniture it may not be necessary to completely pull out all of the old springs or any one of them for that matter, if suitable repairs may be made without this trouble. Sometimes these springs are mounted at one end on pressed metal bars and the nails used to hold these may only be loose, in which event they are pulled out with a pair of pliers and the member shifted a bit so that the nail holes come over fresh wood. The nails are then replaced.

In most instances, it is the webbing in a chair that gives way before the springs. Well anchored springs may last for a long time but webbing, always under strain when a chair is being sat upon, will eventually stretch. This is true of the cheaper forms of non-jute or cotton webbing particularly. If at all possible the worker should purchase only the best which is heavy jute.

In case only the webbing needs pulling up, the following instructions are followed and these, too, may be followed in the case of the total replacement of the webbing.

Fig. 61-A shows how an additional piece of webbing may be pinned to an old piece so that the webbing stretcher may be used. If a simple webbing repair or tightening up job is being made on a chair and no fresh webbing is about, the worker may use a piece of burlap for the spliced piece forming the extension.

However, before the webbing stretcher is employed, it might be well to reinforce the tacking at the opposite end of the webbing using No. 12 tacks. Otherwise, the webbing stretcher may pull the piece away and rip it so that further use will be impossible.

The webbing stretcher is employed as shown in the centre section of Fig. 61. The object of this tool is to pull the webbing up as tightly as possible before tacking. Tacking follows the plan shown in Fig. 61-B. First four No. 12 tacks are driven through the end of the webbing, in a staggered position to prevent splitting the wood. Then about an inch or an inch and a half of material is folded back and tacked again in such a manner that the second row of tacks avoid the first row. Naturally the tacks in the first row are driven in place while the strip of webbing is still under tension imposed by the stretcher. Again the worker is warned against driving these tacks so tightly that their heads cut through the fabric.

If all of the old webbing is in bad shape and needs replacing, the new material is woven in place in the manner shown in Fig. 62.

Aside from old stretched webbing, the most frequent cause of trouble in a chair or sofa is the shifted spring. Thus the worker should strive to anchor the springs to the webbing in the most careful and approved manner as shown in Fig. 62.

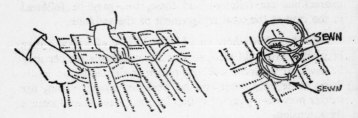

FIG. 62. How webbing is woven (left). Tight weaving is used on bottoms, loose weaving on sides or backs of chairs where there is no strain or weight to support. At right, how webbing it attached to a coiled spring. This is done in four places.

Regular upholsterers' stitching twine is used for this purpose and the ends are tied at least three times over. This method is much better than stitching over the spring end all the way around. Then if the twine breaks at any point the spring will shift.

The reader will quickly understand that every chair or sofa, because of its peculiar shape or construction, has both its own re-covering problem and its own re-upholstery problem.

Therefore it cannot be expected that the exact and detailed procedures used on all types of chairs or sofas can be given in this book. As a matter of fact, that is not necessary. All that the reader needs to know, if he is about to do a complete job, is the accepted general practice as used on all upholstered articles. There is an accepted manner of installing and tying springs, stuffing, padding, spring cushions, etc.

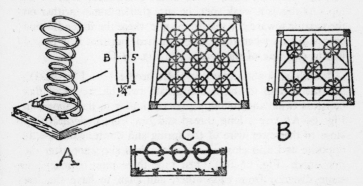

Fig. 63. (A) The method used in holding springs to wood. Small strips of ticking are doubled and tacked over the wire. (B) Method of distributing springs in small and large chair bottoms. (C) How springs are lined up.

For information regarding these skills, the writer knows of no more capable teachers than Miss Florence E. Wright and Miss Charlotte B. Robinson, of the New York State College for Home Economics at Ithaca, New York. The College graciously placed all of its material published by these authors at the disposal of the writer with the permission to use as much of it as he needed. Knowing of no instructions prepared with greater clarity and feeling that this material offered was so much better than he could himself do, the offer made by the College was accepted and the following pages are quoted from this source.

" Either five or nine springs are usually used for a chair seat. They are distributed as shown in Fig. 63-B. So far as possible, place the springs at the crossing of the webbing strips, so that the centres of the springs line up in both directions (Fig. 63-C). Be careful as to the way the spring is turned. The loose end, which bends downward, must be on top. As this is a weak spot, be sure that it comes neither on the outside toward the seat frame nor where the first adjusting cord will pass when the springs are tied, but that it is placed just to one side of the cord, as in Fig. 63-C.

" With an upholsterer's straight needle (see Fig. 61-D) sew tne springs to the webbing with two thicknesses of flax mattress twine and follow a pattern similar to that shown in Fig. 64-A. Use a long thread and sew from underneath up close to the lower wire of the spring and down again exactly opposite and also close to the wire, tie a slip knot after the first stitch (Fig. 65-B). Then take three more stitches the same distance from each other, and plan to have the last stitch near to the next spring.

" A sofa has three or four springs in a row on each slat widthwise and seven or eight lengthwise. In the case of a sofa, place a row of springs near each end and then divide the space so that the centres of the springs will be about $7\frac{1}{2}$ inches apart. To fasten the springs to the board, use two or three pieces of ticking about $1\frac{1}{4}$ by 5 inches (Fig. 63-A). Fold them in half, crosswise, then fold the doubled pieces over the bottom ring of the spring and tack with three No. 8 tacks close to the wire. Place pads of cotton underneath the bottom loose spring wire to prevent it from rattling against the wood.

" A No. 8 steel wire edge is used to give strength between the springs on the front and side edges of a large chair and

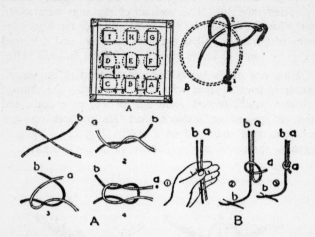

FIGS. 64 and 65. The method of stitching burlap covering to springs (top). Close-up at upper right shows details of knots at 2, 3, 4, etc., in square diagram. Below (A), details of reef knot: (1) Lay one cord on top of the other. The same cord (a) is used to do all the tying. (2) Put the end of cord *a* under the end of cord *b*. (3) Again lay cord *a* on top of *b*. (4) Again put cord *a* under cord *b*. Notice that both ends of each cord come in the same position in relation to the loop formed by the other cord. (B) Slip knot. This is to be used whenever beginning to sew. First take the beginning stitch. Then pull the thread through and leave a short end with which to tie a knot. Lay the long thread with the needle on the table (b). (1) Hold both the long and short ends of cord together. (2) Tie a knot with the short end *a* by laying it on top of the two cords, then pass it under and up in the loop formed by cord *a*. (3) Before tightening the knot, work it down to the end of the short cord so that no twine is wasted. Tighten and pull the long end which draws the knot in place.

of a sofa (Fig. 66) and on all sides of a couch.
The wire is strong and pliable enough to be bent at the corners. A piece of small pipe may be used to bend the wire.

The edge wire should be fastened to the edge springs before the springs are tied. The position of the edge wire at the front when the springs are tied is directly over the front edge of the seat frame. Follow the steps as shown and described in Fig. 63, using 15 inches of double-thickness mattress twine.

" Each row of springs is tied exactly through the centre; first, from back to front on a chair, and across the shortest way of a couch; second, from side to side on a chair, and from end to end on a couch; and last, in both diagonal directions on a chair and on a couch (Fig. 63). Tying is begun on the centre row and the work proceeds outward.

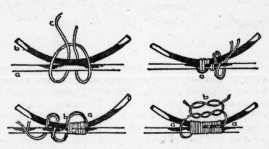

FIG. 66. The method of fastening a spring to a wire edge.

" On all large pieces it is advisable to use extra reinforcements on the outside springs as shown in Fig. 68-B from the tacking at 10 to the back of the spring at 11-K then to 12 where it is tacked. All outside springs are tied on a lower wire in addition to the tying on the top wire. When four or more springs are used, the second spring from the edge is also tied below the top wire (Fig. 69-A-B).

" Always find the centre of the cord and place this point half-way between two opposite sets of tacks. The first time across with the cord, twists are made so that the springs

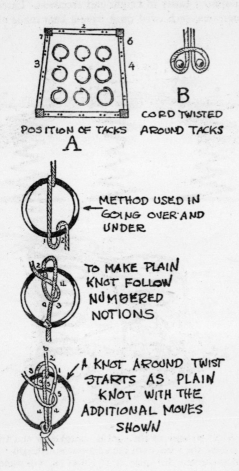

POSITION OF TACKS
A

CORD TWISTED
AROUND TACKS
B

← METHOD USED IN GOING OVER AND UNDER

TO MAKE PLAIN KNOT FOLLOW NUMBERED NOTIONS

A KNOT AROUND TWIST STARTS AS PLAIN KNOT WITH THE ADDITIONAL MOVES SHOWN

Fig. 67. At A and B the method of using tacks for anchoring tying twine is shown. The rest of the drawings show the methods used in making the twists and knots.

may be adjusted easily in height and erectness. Later, as the work progresses, each twist must have a knot made around it

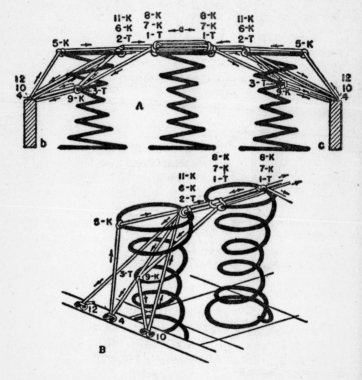

FIG. 68. (A) The centre of the cord is started at *a* and twists (T) are made around the wires until the adjustment of height is correct. The cord is tacked on the frame at 4. Knots (K) are made around the twists and cords are crossed at the centre. (B) the outer springs are tied for extra strength where there are two or three springs in a row. When the diagonal cords from 10 to 11K to 12 are not needed, for example in a small seat with low springs, the cord is fastened at 10.

to keep the cord from slipping. In twisting the cord around the wire, always use *an over and under action* and alternate the side of the end on which the end is brought up (Fig 68).

" With material in hand, follow each direction and observe the diagrams closely.

" Drive two No. 12 tacks side by side into the seat framework directly opposite the centre of each outside spring (Fig. 68). Leave just enough space between the two tacks (Fig. 68) to allow the cord to be wound around each. Drive the tacks far enough into the wood to hold them firm as the cord is pulled around them.

" Measure the cord needed for each row of springs. Lay the cord across the top of the row of springs and allow enough to reach from one set of tacks to the opposite set plus enough extra for fastening it around each set of tacks as shown in Fig. 67. Take three times this measurement. For the additional reinforcement of the outside springs, allow enough more for the diagonal cords from the tacks at 10 in Fig. 68, to knot at 11-K at the back of the first spring and to tacks at 12 plus enough to go around the two sets of tacks and to make the knot. Double the amount of cord used for this reinforcement so that there will be enough for the same reinforcement at the opposite side. This is the amount needed in tying springs from back to front and from side to side.

" For the diagonal tying, measure only one and one-half times the distance to be covered, as this cord crosses the seat only once, with a knot tied where each cord and each wire are crossed.

" Find the centre of the cord. Begin working from the centre of a row of springs (Fig. 68-Aa); run one-half of the cord toward the front (Aa) and one-half toward the back (Ab). Although the work can be done a little more easily by two persons, one standing at the front of the cord, one person can do it alone.

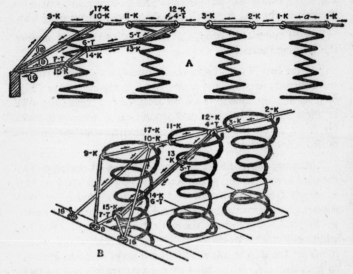

F<small>IG</small>. 69. (A) Tying lengthwise on a sofa. Tying four springs is similar except that the cords are exchanged at the centre. (B) The reinforcement begins at the second spring from the edge and the cord is gradually lowered to the seat frame. The tying of four springs is similar except that the cords are exchanged at the centre.

" Twist the cord over the top wire of each spring, front and back (Fig. 68-A-1-T), except at the front of the edge springs (A-3-T) where the cord should be slanted and twisted over the second or third coil. The reason for this is that if, at this point, the cord were twisted over the top wire, that spring would be forced out of its upright position when the cord was fastened at the edge. By twisting the cord around the second or third wire, the spring stays erect.

" Fasten the cord at the back. To do this, place the cord

between the two tacks (Fig. 67-A-B); twist it around one and brace it against the outside of the other while driving in the first tack. Then place the free end of the cord back in the direction of the springs, but loosely, so that an outward twist may be made and slipped over the second tack. Draw the cord tight and fasten it by driving in the tack.

" Before fastening the cord similarly at the front, adjust the springs to the proper height, either by shortening the cord to lower them or by lengthening it to raise them. Springs should be about 1½ inches lower than the finished chair if no loose cushion is used; and about 3½ inches lower if there is a loose cushion. If a chair has padded arms, the springs are usually tied level with the lower arm and back stretcher.

" If the seat needs to be shaped, as do the Victorian types, adjust the height of the springs at this time.

" After the cord is fastened at the front and back, slip the springs back and forth until they are all erect.

" The worker is now ready to go back over the springs, making knots instead of twists. First, make a knot (Fig. 67) on the front edge of the front spring, then proceed by making knots (Fig. 67) to hold the twists firmly in place.

" For three springs in a row (Fig. 68-Aa-B) carry the cord, after first tacking it to the frame, up and over the front of the top wire of the front spring and thence to the back of the same wire, and knot over the twist at that point (Fig. 68-6-K).

" Next, carry the cord to the first twist on the middle spring and make a knot over it (7-K over 1-T) leave that cord, and repeat the process with the back cord. Cross the two cords over the middle spring so that the one coming from the back is used to complete the tying at the front springs of the seat and the cord from the front is used for the back springs. Make a knot, 8-K, over the knot already at each side of the middle spring. Next, carry the cord to the lower twist on the front spring (Fig. 68-3-T), make a knot (Fig. 68-9-K) and then draw the cord to the edge of the frame in a wide angle and fasten it as shown in Fig. 67 with two tacks at B. For the diagonal reinforcements, carry the cord up to the back of the front spring in such a way that it will not rub on a wire as the chair is used, and make another knot around the knot already there (Fig. 68-11-K). As this knot is formed it is important to go *over* the wire on the opposite side from that on which the cord was tacked, to prevent the knot from slipping. After the knot is made, brace the cord by going *over* the wire on the opposite side from where it will be tacked (Fig. 68-12) and then carry the cord to the edge of the frame as directly as possible and in such a way that this cord will not be rubbed by the wires. Fasten it there with two tacks.

" For two springs in a row carry the cord, after first tacking it to the edge of the frame, up and over the front of the top wire of the front spring, and knot it there for the first and only time (Fig. 67).

" Thence carry it to the twist made at the back of the same wire (Fig. 70-5-K) and knot it over the twist on that point. Repeat this process at the back and cross cords so that the cord from the back is used to make a knot at 6-K at the front (Fig. 70-A); then proceed to the frame and tack it there, using the method described in Fig. 67. Likewise, use the cord from the front to make knot 6-K, Fig. 70, at the back and then tack it to the back frame.

" For one spring this process is used in a grouping of five springs, with two at the sides and a single spring at the centre, or for a seat with three springs. Always tie the springs in a row first, following directions previously given to establish the height. For a single spring, start the cord on the second or third wire below the top. Twist each half-length of the cord over the opposite sides of this wire and draw it, to front and back, respectively, for fastening. Before the front is fastened, however, adjust this single spring to the correct height for the rest of the springs. After making the cord fast around the tacks at both ends, bring back the halves of the cord to the top of the spring, and knot them there, once in front and once in back. Cross the cord ends and knot each one over the twist first made on the lower wire. Fasten the cords on the edge of the frame by twisting them around the two tacks as shown in Fig. 67.

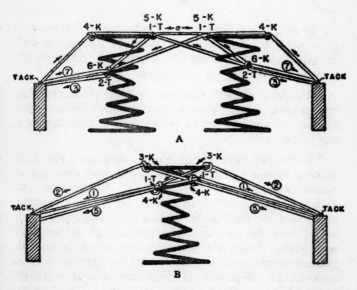

FIG. 70. How a double spring (A) is tied and how a single spring (B) is tied.

" For large chairs and couches that have four or more springs, a strong reinforcement is needed along the edge. Begin as described previously at the centre row of springs and work toward the front or toward the back. When the second row from the edge is reached, make a twist as usual over the back of the top wire, then, instead of making a twist at the front of that wire, lower the cord to the coil just below and make a twist at the front of that wire (5-T). Make the next twist on the back of the third coil of the edge spring (6-T), then another on the front of the fourth coil of that spring (7-T). This will keep the springs steady and in place.

" The knotting is done exactly as for three springs in a row.

" In tying couch, davenport or chaise-lounge springs, first tie across in the short direction (widthwise), beginning with the centre row and working toward each end. Adjust all the rows to the height of the centre one.

" Because of the wire edge used on large pieces, the edge springs on all sides of a couch must be pulled forward when tied, so that this wire will be exactly over the front edge of a seat frame.

" In the lengthwise direction of a couch there are seven or eight springs. If the couch is open at each end, special reinforcement is needed (Fig. 69-A-B). Measure the cord as described previously. Start from the centre with the middle of the cord and work toward each end, knotting around each wire crossed and twisting around the cord in the centre of each spring. When the next-to-the-end spring is reached, proceed as previously described for reinforcing four or more springs. Tie diagonally in both directions as explained previously and as shown.

" The next step is to cover the springs with burlap. Select a firm closely-woven burlap and lay it over the top of the springs, with the grain straight from the centre front and from side to side. Cut it to hang about two inches over the top of the seat frame. To make the material fit around the leg posts, follow the directions given in Fig. 71 and leave about 1½ inches to turn under as cuts b and c are made. Turn up the edges of the burlap twice, so that the folds are on the outside, and tack the folded edge to the top edge of the seat frame.

Do not pull the burlap so tightly that the springs are depressed.

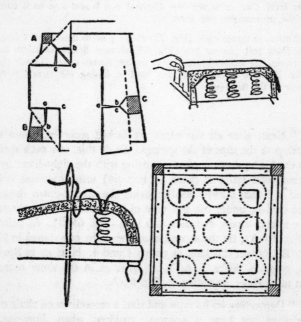

Figs. 71, 72, 73 and 74. Upper left (A). When material is cut to one corner of a post and is fitted the same way on two sides of the post: Pull the material as tight as it will be when the work is completed. Find the point where it meets the inner corner of the post at the level of the seat and mark this point with pencil or pin. Fold back the corner of the material as shown. First make a diagonal slash (a) from the outside corner of the cloth to the corner of the post. Then make the two slashes b and c, following the grain of the material to within an inch to an inch and a half of the end of the first cut so as to allow enough to turn under. (B) When enough material is needed to be drawn around the front posts: Follow the grain of material cutting it at a, until the cut meets an imaginary line from the corner of the cloth (c) to the corner of the post, then make diagonal cut b to meet the corner of the post. (C) When the material is cut to fit around two corners: Fold the material back close to the post. Make cut a, on the grain leading to centre of the post, to within an inch and a half of the post at the seat level, then make the two diagonal cuts b and c to each corner of the post at the seat level.

Sketch at upper right (Fig. 72) shows how to determine shape of the front roll. Lower left (Fig. 73) pictures details of stitch used to fasten the second burlap cover to first burlap cover. Lower right (Fig. 74) is diagram of stitches used in sewing the second burlap cover to the first one.

" Next, after all the edges are tacked securely, fasten the burlap to the tops of the springs. To do this, sew each spring to the burlap in four places, starting with the right-hand front spring and tying at point 1 (Fig. 64) using mattress twine and a 6-inch curved needle: Bring the needle down through the burlap, under the top wire of the spring and up through the burlap again, and tie a slip knot (Fig. 65-B). At point 2 (Fig. 64-A), tie the second knot, using the one shown in Fig. 65-B. Repeat this knot at points 3 and 4. Next go to Spring B, tying at points 5, 6, 7, 8; continue in the same manner on all springs, as shown in Fig. 64-A.

" Depending on its type and size, a reconditioned chair may or may not have a separate cushion; when, however, a separate cushion is planned, the padding of the seat is done differently.

" On top of the first piece of burlap place the padding (hair or moss). Pull and fluff each handful well before placing it on the top of the seat; this procedure makes the final seat softer and more springy. This layer of padding should take the shape of the finished seat. Cover the burlap, both top and sides, so deeply that, when pressed down by the hands, the padding is about two inches thick over the tops of the springs and thicker around the edges.

" Stitch the padding to the burlap, using a curved needle and mattress twine. Thread the needle without cutting the twine from the ball, and sew with big loose stitches, placing the final stitch close to the first one. Beginning at the first stitch and continuing to the last one, pull each stitch tightly; this tightening makes the padding more compact and thus firmer. Next, make a tight knot of the two ends and cut the twine from the ball. With this method less twine is needed than when separate pieces are used.

" Lay a second piece of burlap over the padding and temporarily pin it in place. This piece should be large enough to cover the padding and to hang down over all four sides of the seat frame. To determine the shape of the front padding, which will differ from that on the sides, stand in front of the chair, take hold of the edge of the hanging material and hold it out horizontally and in line with the top of the chair seat, and with the other hand, grasp it between the thumb and fingers at a point directly above the frame so that the material drops in a vertical position and in line with the front seat frame (Fig. 72). Cut off this hanging material about two inches below the top of the frame; then cut out the corners around the arm supports as directed in Fig. 71.

" With a few tacks, temporarily fasten the burlap to the frame at the four corners. Begin with the front and back and then do the sides; keep the grain of the material straight in both directions. The burlap can be easily slipped on and off these tacks as adjustment is needed. The material between the corners should be left loose enough to insert more padding if needed. To obtain a better tacking surface for this part of the work, bevel with a rasp the top edge of the frame.

" Without cutting the mattress twine from the ball, thread
a double-pointed needle with it. Make a slip at one corner,
then insert the needle, drawing the eye through only the first
layer of burlap and approximately through the centre of the
corner spring. Without drawing the eye lower, push it up,
close to where it went down, avoiding all springs and cords.
About 4 inches from this point, put the needle down and
back again in a similar manner (Fig. 73). Continue until a
complete row has been loosely sewed all around the edges,
having the stitches come on a line with the centre of the
outside springs. Pull the stitches tight and tie as described
previously. Next, make two or more rows of stitches in the
centre as shown in Fig. 74.

" Insert padding in the back and sides of the seat until they
are the desired shape. Tuck the edge of the burlap under the
stuffing and pin it temporarily to the first burlap with upholstery pins. Make any adjustments needed by adding more
padding or by moving the padding with the regulator until
the edges are firm and smooth. Now replace the pins with
tacks.

" When filling and stitching the front edge of the seat,
complete the stuffing at the front. Tuck the loose burlap under
the padding, and fasten it temporarily in place with upholstery
pins. This front stuffing should be firm and flat across the
top and the front. It then will be flush with the front of the
frame. Use the regulator to shape this stuffing.

" To hold this padding firmly in place, stitch it with
mattress twine. Depending on the height of the padding
above the frame and the amount of firmness needed, select
one of the stitches shown at bottom of Fig. 75. On a large
chair seat, a combination of stitches is used; those that make
a small edge roll protect the edge of the seat, and the long
stitches hold the top and the front firmly in place.

" To plan the place for the stitches that make the edge roll,

pinch up the edge with the fingers at the place that seems most suitable, then put a pencil or crayon mark where the fingers come. Usually, this is about 1 inch above and below the seat edge. With a yardstick and pencil, draw lines across the seat at these two places as a guide for the stitches. Then on the top, draw the two lines that show where to take the long stitches that hold the top of the front padding flat (Fig. 75). The first line can be about ½ inch behind the line planned for the edge roll. The second line is placed back from the edge as far as possible without meeting the stitching on top of the seat. Finally, draw the two lines across the front of the seat padding: The first about ½ inch below the edge roll stitch; and the second as low as stitches can be taken; this usually is about ½ inch above the seat frame.

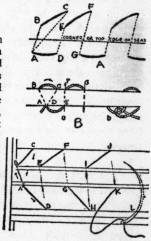

FIG. 75. Method at top is used when the edge padding is shallow, as on a Victorian side chair or when added firmness is needed on the shallow edges of a back or sides of a seat. Method sketched at centre is used alone to give more firmness than preceding method, and always with that illustrated at bottom on the front of a large chair where it is necessary to have an edge that will stand a great deal of wear. Bottom method is used to hold firmly the top and front of a large edge padding.

"Thread a 6-inch curved needle with mattress twine. Follow Fig. 75-B to stitch first the edge roll. Use the regulator to push the padding firmly into this edge so that when stitched the burlap is full of padding. Start at the left and make the stitches about ¾ inch apart, first put the needle in at the lower line and stitch through to the top line at B, slightly behind where it went in at A, holding the end of the twine so that it will not slip through; then put the needle in at C, and bring it out on the lower line at A, make a slip knot there to fasten the thread. Continue stitching across the front. Each time the twine comes out at the lower line, slip the needle through the last loop (b) and draw the cord first backward, then forward to tighten it.

" Thread the long straight needle with mattress twine and follow diagram at bottom of Fig. 75 to make the stitches on top and at the front. The curved needle may be used if the distance is not too great for it to reach. Begin at the left side at A just below the edge roll, then stitch through to the front line on top near the edge roll at B slightly below where it went in at A. Hold the end of the thread so that it will not slip through. Then insert the needle at C, bring it out at A, and make a slip knot there. Continue the stitches across the seat; insert the needle at D, bring it out at E; insert the needle in F at the back of the top and let the needle come out in front at G; continue across and fasten the twine. The twine should be pulled tight as the stitches are made, and the regulator should be used constantly to make the padding firm and smooth.

" For seats with separate cushions or without a wire edge, proceed as follows: Directly over the first burlap, lay a second piece large enough to hang down about 2 inches below the top of the seat frame except at the front, where it should hang below the bottom. Make sure that the grain of the burlap runs straight from front to back and from side to side, then pin the piece temporarily at the four corner springs. With the curved needle and mattress twine, stitch the two pieces of burlap together, making the line of stitches approximately through the centre of the top of the outside springs (Fig. 76).

" Next, at the back and sides, fasten the burlap temporarily in place with tacks at the corners. Insert between the first and second burlap enough hair or moss to make a firm and well-shaped padding over the edges, then turn the upper piece of burlap under the padding; first pin it in place with upholstery pins, and then tack it to the top edge of the frame.

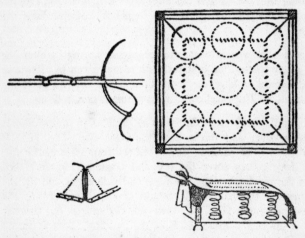

FIGS. 76, 77, 78 and 79. Upper left, details of stitch used to sew burlap to a wire edge. Upper right, diagram of stitches used in sewing the second burlap cover to the first burlap cover in a chair with loose cushions. Lower left, method used in folding burlap under the corners. Lower right, determining the shape of the front roll for a chair having a loose cushion. The front roll should slant upward.

" Before padding the front, hold the loose burlap forward and slanting upward. Pinch a spot between thumb and fingers directly above the front of the frame and let the rest of the burlap drop down parallel with it (Fig. 77), then cut off the extra material about 2 inches below the top of the frame. Fill the front space with padding, making it slant from the seat upwards toward the outside. When this space is firm and well-filled, tuck the burlap under the padding; first pin it in place with upholstery pins, and then tack it to the top edge of the front of the frame.   Stitch the roll, following the directions given in Fig. 75-B-C. Make sure to keep the roll slanting upward to give an edge that will hold the cushion in place and constantly use the regulator to help shape the edge."

In case the worker wishes to reconstruct spring cushions, he can do no better than follow the directions given by Charlotte B. Robinson, also of the New York State College of Home Economics. The excellent advice of this expert follows:

" Rip the back and side seams of the bottom of the outside cushion cover and throw back the loose flap (Fig. 80). If narrow strips of padding lie around the four sides of the unit and large pieces cover the top and bottom (Fig. 81) then open the top layer along the back and side edges and lift the springs. If the padding is wound several times around the inner spring unit (Fig. 82), then pull the springs out through one of the easily-opened ends of the padding. Before tearing the unit apart, be sure to count and make a note of the number of springs in each row, and of the number of rows from back to front and from side to side, so that the new springs may be placed in the same order. If the material covering the springs is badly torn and the springs are more or less tangled, pull them apart, count them, and determine the number that should be in each row. All springs should be of the same height and should stand erect; if not, pull all the bent ones into shape.

" The new unit will be made from several long cases of

stout, non-stretching material, such as muslin, seed-bags, or burlap, to contain the pockets for the springs. When filled, these are tied together.

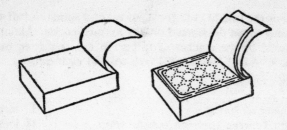

FIGS. 80 and 81. Left, back and side seams of a spring cushion open. Right, spring cushion with top layer of padding turned back.

"Figure the size of the piece for each case: Write down the measurements needed and figure the width and length of the piece to be used for each row of springs.

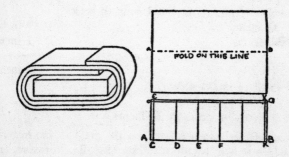

FIGS. 82 and 83. Left, padding wound around inner spring units. Right, upper sections shows cut-off on measured strip. Lower diagram shows cut-off measured strip folded in half and marked for stitching.

" For the width: Add the diameter of a spring to the height of the side wall of the outside cushion cover between the cordings, plus $\frac{1}{2}$ inch for the seam. Multiply the total by 2.

" For the length: Add the diameter of a spring to half the diameter to get the amount needed for each pocket. Multiply this total by the number of springs in one row from front to back. Add 1 inch for a $\frac{1}{2}$ inch seam at each end.

For example:

Width of Piece

Diameter of spring	3 inches
Height between cords on outside cover	$3\frac{1}{2}$ inches
Seam	$\frac{1}{2}$ inch
	7 inches

$2 \times 7 = 14$ inches

Length of Piece

Diameter of spring	3 inches
$\frac{1}{2}$ diameter of spring	$1\frac{1}{2}$ inches
Each pocket	$4\frac{1}{2}$ inches
6 (number of pockets in 1 row front to back) $\times$ $4\frac{1}{2}$ inches =	27 inches
2 $\frac{1}{2}$-inch seams	1 inch
	28 inches

Each piece 14 inches wide
28 inches long
Need 5 pieces 14 inches by 28 inches.

" Cut off the measured strip on the grain of the material and fold it in half, lengthwise (Fig. 83-A-B). Measure, and mark with pencil lines, $\frac{1}{2}$ inch in from each edge; then stitch on these lines (Fig. 83-C, C, XX). Starting from the seam, CC, mark off the width of one pocket at point D (Fig. 83), draw a line from that point parallel to the seam and stitch along this line. Now fit a spring in this pocket to see whether it is on the right size, inserting it as shown in Fig. 84, and turning it as in Fig. 85. Although non-stretchable material is recommended, stretchable material may have to be used. *If the width has stretched* so that the spring is loose in the pocket, place a pin to take up the extra width and mark this point with a pencil. Remove the spring and the stitching, mark a new line with a pencil, and stitch along it. To find whether the material has stretched in height, first put a series of pins across the top of the spring on the planned line (Fig. 83, O, O) after the spring has been inserted and turned as in Fig. 85. If the measurement is more than that planned (the same as the height of the outside cushion cover between cords), lower the pins the distance needed to make the measurement correct. Mark this position with a pencil at one point; remove the pins and the spring; measure the distance from the bottom of the case to the marked point and use this measurement for drawing line O-O (Fig. 83).

" It is important to measure from the bottom up, thus ensuring the same height for each pocket and letting any irregularity come at the top seam.

" Press the springs flat, insert them sidewise into the pockets, pushing each spring to the bottom (Fig. 84). To hold the springs in place, insert a pin close to each spring; to hold the two sides of the case together, insert two or three pins at right angles to the edges. Stitch on the line marked J-K (Figs. 84 and 85). And remove the pins. Then turn the springs at right angles, so they will be upright in the pockets, with the seam running through the middle of the spring tops (Fig. 85-J-K).

" Arrange the filled cases with the long sides together (Fig. 86-A) and fasten them by tying the tops and bottoms of the springs right through the cloth as follows: thread a curved or straight needle with mattress twine, kite twine, or strong pliable parcel twine and have the length 1½ times the distance to be sewn. Insert it through the cloth and under the top wire of an outside spring (Fig. 86-A-a). Tie a slip knot (Fig. 86-A). Then continue by passing the needle through the material and under *two* adjacent top wires of each pair of springs, using the knot shown at A-d. End the row with a square knot (Fig. 86-C). Tie each row in the same way from side to side and then repeat the tying from back to front (Fig. 87). Turn the unit over and tie the bottom side in the same way. Another way would be to tie the top and bottom of each single row, and then assemble them into a unit.

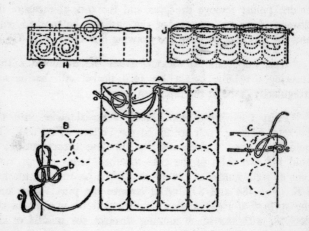

FIGS. 84, 85 and 86. Upper left, how springs are dropped into pockets sidewise and, upper right, how they are turned upright in pockets. Below, how filled cases are fastened together. Left, a slip knot—tie with short end b and draw thread up to cloth with long end c. Right, a square knot. Tie knot at C as at A, d. Then tie knot f.

" To replace the finished spring unit in a cushion that has an open flap (Fig. 81) lay it back in the padding in its former place without crushing the side pads. See that this side padding is pulled up around the sides of the spring unit and that it is of the same thickness all the way around and is smooth on the outside. Draw the loose, top padding back over the spring unit. To insert the spring unit into the cushion that has padding wound around (Fig. 82) bend the sides of the unit inward, push it through the hole at the end of the padding, then flatten the unit.

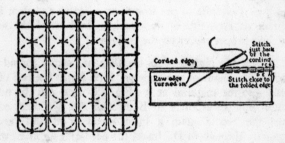

FIGS. 87 and 88. Diagram at left shows pockets fastened together and tied. Right, how pinned edges of the cover are sewn together.

" In both types of cushions, make the corners square and well-filled; cover any holes in the padding by laying pieces of upholsterer's cotton felt under them or place a new layer over the entire top. If this material is not available, use layers of cotton batting or an old cotton blanket, quilt, mattress pad, or some similar material.

" If new cotton is to be used, lay two or three thicknesses of cotton felt (enough so that the springs cannot be felt by the hand from the outside) in the bottom of the outside cushion cover and let the cotton cover also the four sides; lay the spring unit in place; cover the top of the spring unit with the same amount of cotton felt and let this piece extend also over the sides. This makes two or more thicknesses of cotton over the top and four or more filling in the space between the outside cover and the spring unit. Add more if it is needed to fill entirely the side spaces.

" Pull the loose top of the cushion cover back into place. Make sure that all raw edges are turned in and that the cording, when present, is stitched securely to the edge of the loose-cushion cover top. Pin the open edges together first at the corners, then at the middle of the back and the middle of the sides. Continue to pin first from a centre and then from a corner on each side of the cushion. Pull all of the seams into their proper places on the cushion.

" To sew the pinned edges together, use carpet thread that matches the colour of the cushion. First fasten the end of the thread into the material at A (Fig. 88) then run the needle straight upward from A to B through the two open edges. Insert the needle again a little ahead of B and push it diagonally through to D. Insert the needle again at E, which is a little behind D. Repeat sewing as from A. The completed cushion should look flat, should have square corners and be firm and comfortable."